D0921620

INTRODUCTION TO MACROECONOMIC THEORY

EDWARD AMES
PURDUE UNIVERSITY

Holt, Rinehart and Winston
NEW YORK CHICAGO SAN FRANCISCO ATLANTA
DALLAS MONTREAL TORONTO LONDON

Library of Congress Catalog Card Number: 68–21732
2691459
Printed in the United States of America
1 2 3 4 5 6 7 8 9

PREFACE

For twenty years, the standard dose of macroeconomic theory in the standard principles of economics course has consisted of (a) a two-equation, two-variable linear theory of the national income; and (b) a literary description of the multiple expansion of bank reserves. These two propositions are analytically unrelated. To them an institutional and intuitive description of a few issues in fiscal and monetary policy is normally adjoined.

Today, of course, professional economists have ceased to be interested in this particular pair of analytical propositions—they have learned a good deal in the past twenty years. The main thrust of modern macroeconomic writing (apart from the literature on growth models) has to do with the unification of income and monetary theory. This unification has proceeded on various fronts. In social accounting, Copeland has developed moneyflows analysis, which relates the income accounts to the financial markets. Gurley and Shaw have supplemented the older analysis of banking institutions with the treatment of financial intermediaries. Tobin and others have been concerned with the problems of portfolio selection at the macroeconomic level. Monetary writers as varied as Friedman, Horwich, Modigliani, and Patinkin have all sought to combine the study of income determination with the study of capital markets with a precision and refinement that was undreamed of when Wicksell, Fisher, and Keynes wrote the material which is the foundation of the present sophomore course.

Because the macroeconomic content of the usual sophomore textbook is not in the spirit of contemporary work, it has become a bore to teachers and therefore to their students. The main obstacle to improving this particular piece of the sophomore course has been the absence of a simple, but comprehensive way of combining the income and balance sheet approaches to economics. Such a comprehensive approach is available, if advantage is taken of the course in finite mathematics, which has become a standard part of freshman curricula. For this course gives the notation and the basic reasoning necessary to enable the construction of rather interesting, but elementary macroeconomic theories. It is not wise to teach mathematics in economics courses, but it is easy to use the notation in this, the simplest of college mathematics courses, to develop the basic themes of income and monetary theory. Students who have gone "the calculus route" in their required mathematics have no serious problems with finite mathematics, for finite mathematics is easier than calculus.

This short book introduces macroeconomics from the point of view of income and capital markets. It deals with theories concerned with both national income and balance sheet accounts. The theories are all constructed in linear form so they can be understood by students who have taken a standard freshman course in finite mathematics. Because the emphasis is on economics and not mathematics, the book does not require students actually to perform many calculations, although it does explain what calculations are performed. Because the treatment is systematic, the income and the monetary theories are presented in the same form. Consequently, the usual divergence in style between monetary and income economics can be avoided, and the two systems may readily be compared.

Even in a simple, linear context, it is possible to present some of the central issues of contemporary economics. These issues reflect the fact that some economists approach their subject from the background of income determination, while others approach it from the background of monetary analysis. Indeed, most of the controversy in this area is between those who regard the stock of money and the demand for assets as the basic determinants of economic life, and those who regard the demand for current output as the basic determinants of economic life. If the world could be represented by linear systems, it would be possible to associate each view with a particular collection of matrix equations; some economists choose to set one group of coefficients in a matrix equal to zero, and others set a different group of coefficients equal to zero. When we set up theories for beginners, it is natural to set forth in just that way what the different theories say, for in this way their mechanics can be easily compared.

Of course, it is a great simplification to use only linear theories, and certain problems cannot readily be discussed. For instance, a linear theory cannot have a declining marginal propensity to consumer. It does not easily handle prices (although the interest rate is no great problem). But if all interesting problems could be solved in a few weeks, there would be no need for advanced courses, and most of us would be without jobs.

A macroeconomic theory is a proposed explanation of the behavior of some part of the social accounts. It is natural to start with a schematic consideration of the logic of social accounting in Chapter 2: What are income accounts; what are balance sheets; how are they related; and how are they aggregated? It is also natural to consider what a theory is (Chapter 3): what do theories tell us, and how is one constructed?

The economic substance of the book consists of a sequence of theories. Chapter 4 gives three familiar theories about the national product, and Chapter 5 gives two familiar theories about the banking system and the interest rate. These last theories are familiar in the sense that their conclusions are familiar. They are unfamiliar, perhaps, in form because banking theories are ordinarily presented to sophomores in literary form, although they could just as easily be presented as formal models.

Chapter 6 is concerned with a very simple "moneyflows" model. There are income, nonbank balance sheet and bank balance sheet accounts. The chapter discusses how the parts must be put together if a coherent system is to be obtained. More interesting perhaps, from the student's point of view, is the fact that several rather different theories can be presented using basically the same skeleton. In one version, income generation is the motive force; in another, money is the motive force; in a third, money is "neutral," being quite independent of both income and the demand for plant. These variants make it possible to see why theorists may reach rather different conclusions about economic policies, and about the underlying mechanism of economic events. Each variant makes (I think) plausible assumptions about consumer and business behavior. The fact that such different theories can plausibly be formulated explains the need for empirical analysis, which is the subject matter of other books in this series.

Undergraduates (and teachers) seem to enjoy discussions of fiscal and monetary policy. These discussions can usefully be based upon the growing literature on welfare economics. Chapter 7, therefore, introduces the notion of Pareto optimality. Although this notion is more commonly reserved for microeconomics, it has relevance for macroeconomics. After all, if the economy is working at less than "capacity," a way exists to make everyone better off. If it is working at capacity, changes in the consumption-investment ratio affect the relation between present and future consumption. Both fiscal and monetary policies have welfare implications. The general procedure used in the book means that the "mechanics" of fiscal and monetary policy are discussed first, and the welfare discussion builds upon knowledge of these results.

The problem in teaching economic theory these days is to keep economic content from being swamped in mathematical detail. The systematic use of linear methods makes it possible to avoid teaching mathematics, other than notation. Assumptions about the social accounts and about economic behavior can ordinarily be written down as simple mapping of endogenous variables into exogeneous variables (called "factors" in this book). Inversion of this mapping gives a mapping of exogenous into endogenous variables. Matrix inversion is a tedious chore, which students do not actually have to carry out to use this book. They do have to understand what is done; this is explained in Chapter 3. They are also given a rule for verifying that the inversion has been done correctly. Given the inverse matrix, one can prepare a table directly which shows the effect of a unit change in each exogenous variable on each endogenous variable. Such a table is given as an interpretation of each theory presented.

Because there is a "standard procedure," the mathematics of a theory are subordinated to the economic content, as is proper. But because a "standard procedure" can be developed, students can be given a wider variety of subject matter than in the traditional method. Theories in the professional literature involve several variables, and more or less subtle connections among them. Empirical work involves basically deciding when one theory is better than another. Economists are concerned with ideas (in the plural), and they have to combine them in such a way as to produce coherence. When they encounter difficulties (as usually happens) they must consider different ways of dealing with them.

Two chapters in this book may present a problem to teachers using it for the first time. The first is Chapter 3, the second is Chapter 6. In Chapter 3, one group of students (those of scientific bent) will find it very simple to perform the operation of rewriting a set of equations in vector-matrix form. Another group, however, may panic because symbols appear. If too little time is spent on Chapter 3, the second group will have trouble with the rest of the book. If too much, the first group will lose interest. Teachers, then, should try to make students actually write out and perform simple matrix operations in class, as soon as Chapter 3 is reached. But they should not make the mistake of continuing this exercise very long. Students can practice this operation by themselves more efficiently than in class, once they have seen it done a few times under supervision. If too much time is spent on Chapter 3 in class, the effect seems to be to persuade the timid that the material is more difficult than it actually is.

The problem in Chapter 6 is related to that in Chapter 3. A new element exists, however. Students are evidently accustomed to being given "the word," and they expect to be told which of the four versions of the theory in that chapter was actually brought down from Mount Sinai. Teachers are welcome, of course, to tell them. The author's message, however, is a different one: The profession disagrees about how the economy works, and it is possible to set up literate, but conflicting theories.

Chapter 6 aims, at expressing precisely but simply the differences among the theories. It should, therefore, be an analytical basis for using any of the numerous "readings" volumes in the market. These "readings" usually consist of testimony at Congressional hearings, speeches, and the like. They present emotions and sometimes conclusions based on analysis. They seldom present analysis. Chapter 6 shows how, by suitably selecting one's assumptions, one can derive a considerable variety of conclusions. (Theories 2 and 3 in Chapter 4 do the same thing.) The author has found it hard to use "readings" in the principles course because the usual textbook discussion of macreoeconomic theory presents only the author's favorite model. This book aims at variety of models but consistency of technique.

In order to achieve this purpose, teachers using Chapter 6 must devote some time to comparing the four versions of the theory. This comparison, from the technical point of view, involves looking at four matrices and seeing that each of them contains certain blocks of zeros and certain nonzero elements. These, of course, correspond to different assertions about how the economy works. As in Chapter 3, the pedagogical problem is to spend enough time, but not too much in class, on "mechanics".

Economists differ a good deal about their concept of equilibrium. Some say the economy is always in equilibrium. Others say it is never in equilibrium but always seeking equilibrium. In part, the difference is definitional. In this book, mainly for purposes of exposition, the discussion proceeds *as if* the economy was always in equilibrium, even though shifts in exogenous factors may mean that there is continual change in the equilibrium point.

This point of view cuts away the need for certain kinds of discussion which confuses beginners. The existing texts tend to define equilibrium as a solution to a set of equations (Tiny Model 1, in this book). Then they ask, "Suppose there were not equilibrium, what would happen?" Students naturally inquire, "Why talk about equilibrium at all if it does not occur?"

Books of theory, especially for beginners, should try to present theory as a way of producing coherence, and as a way of setting forth alternative possibilities. For such books are about ideas. They should not pretend to certainty on matters where the profession is uncertain. They should, however, present any idea in a way that explores its implications. The author's problem has been to combine precision of analysis with variety of conceptual structure.

This book is a simplified version of a longer and more advanced text, *Income and Wealth*, published by Holt, Rinehart and Winston. In that book, more attention is paid to calculation. A variety of applications are presented as problems. Teachers using this shortened version may find it useful, in organizing classroom work, to consult the longer version for suggestions of topics which can be discussed in class.

I should like to thank Keith Brown and Hugo Sonnenschein for trying out early versions of this book on groups of undergraduates. Chiou-shuang Yan gave the final draft a careful reading, and has spared me embarrassment at several points. The remaining errors are strictly my own. I should also like to thank Betty Morris for typing the manuscript in its several forms and for her help in putting it into coherent and printable form.

West Lafayette, Indiana
April 1968

Edward Ames

CONTENTS

1

INTRODUCTION

Economics studies production and exchange of goods and services. The problem is to explain what goods and how many goods get made, what kinds of income, and how large incomes are earned, what kinds of wealth and how much wealth are available in a community. Over a period of time, the problem is to explain why certain groups become "better off"—either because they can buy more than formerly, or because their position has improved relative to other groups. The subject is classified according to the size of the groups considered in particular problems. *Microeconomics* (from the Greek word *mikros*, meaning *small*) is concerned with small groups and even individuals. *Macroeconomics* (from the Greek word *makros*, meaning *large*) deals with large groups, and in some cases, entire countries. In this book, the point of view is resolutely macroeconomic.

Consider two examples of macroeconomic events. The output of consumer goods in the United States has shown a steady tendency to rise more rapidly than population. The standard of living, which is simply the ratio (consumer goods/people), has therefore risen. In many other countries, the standard of living has not risen. Why is it that in some countries the standard of living rises and in other ones it does not?

In the United States during the 1930s, as everyone knows, at least one fifth of the labor force was unemployed at any one time—something that has never happened before or since. There are practical reasons for studying this national disaster: Another such period of mass unemployment would be most unpleasant for us all. So long as we do not know why that period took place, we cannot be sure that another might not occur, or what might be done about it. Mass unemployment is a macroeconomic phenomenon.

The United States has never had something which economists call a hyperinflation. In Germany in 1923, prices rose to levels of approximately one billion times as high as those in 1920. In mid-1946, prices in Hungary rose to levels 10^{56} times as high as at the end of 1944. The closest we have come to hyperinflation was during the Civil War, when prices in the Confederacy rose to levels which seemed at the time astronomical, although that rise has been "outdone" in many other countries. Hyperinflations are macroeconomic events.

Within more normal experience, unemployment increases and decreases, but (in the United States) it remains in a range of 3–6 percent of the labor force, and prices rise or fall at most a few percent a year. Macroeconomics, therefore, usually deals with relatively small-scale changes in the way people live. These changes, however, are real, and make a noticeable difference to large groups in the community. Over a period of even ten years, these small changes may cumulate into large changes.

This book presents a way of looking at macroeconomic events and gives a series of applications of the basic method to several macroeconomic topics. Any branch of learning is based upon a systematic classification of events, and of the interrelations among them. In the following chapters, such a classification is developed and used. Chapter 2 shows that the terms "income" and "wealth" correspond to two basic classifications of macroeconomics. In Chapter 3 we discuss what a macroeconomic theory should do, and in later chapters we construct a number of theories about income and wealth.

To say that one has constructed a theory does not necessarily mean that one has constructed a good theory. The test of a good theory lies in showing that it fits the facts. But there is no way to test a theory if there is no theory to test. Economists are never in a position to say that a theory fits the data perfectly; and they can seldom say that the theory is completely bad. The usual situation is that a theory has some good and some bad features. Progress takes place when a theory is improved, even if perfection is not attained.

In some natural sciences, it is possible to test a theory by experimental means. Economists are not able to perform controlled experiments. Therefore, they must confine themselves to the careful study of the past, so as to determine whether what has happened is consistent with their theories. To a considerable extent, this testing involves the use of complicated statistical methods. There are many cases, indeed, where a superficial examination of the record lends some support to all sides in a dispute. Because the testing of theories involves special techniques different from those involved in formulating theories, this book does not deal with the question of deciding which, if any, are most applicable to the United States economy of the 1960s and 1970s.

Short of performing statistical tests, however, there are some ways of evaluating theories. One way is to ask how many phenomena the theory can explain. We shall present theories that deal just with the national income, and others that deal only with the banking system. We can say that the last group of theories (in Chapter 6) is better than the theories in (say) Chapters 4 or 5, because they deal with the national income and the monetary system as a single, interrelated unit.

Another way to evaluate theories is in terms of the variety of behavior they represent. In Chapter 4, three theories are presented. In one of these (Theory 2), decisions by businesses as to how much expansion they will undertake are held to be completely unrelated to the current state of the economy. In another (Theory 3), businesses are said to take into account the level of consumer spending, the amount of taxes they are currently paying, and the level of government spending. Thus Theory 3 takes into account a wider range of possible business behavior, and yields interesting suggestions as to the ways in which government can affect the economy. In this sense, it is "better than" Theory 2, even if we do not know whether it is true or not.

Consequently, if any theory in this book were represented as "true" it would be misleading. Rather, each theory is a proposal which is (we hope) better than the previous one, but not so good as the next one. This is a book for beginners, in a subject about which much remains to be learned. It points the reader in the right direction, leads him a few steps, and pushes him off on his own. If the reader has mastered the basic method, he may be able to take a step by himself.

A theory consists of several kinds of propositions. One kind specifies the structure of some portion of the economy. Another kind asserts how some group is believed to use its income or its wealth. The second group of propositions refers to *allocation of resources*, which is one name for the central analytical problem posed by economics: Granted a limited income, what determines the uses to which it will be put; granted a limited amount of wealth, how will this wealth be used?

The typical statement about allocation takes the following form: The amount of income devoted to a particular use (for example, purchases of consumer goods) depends on the total amount of income available for all uses; or the amount of wealth that will be held in any particular form (for example, cash) depends on the total wealth. This particular kind of statement enables us to make theories without too much trouble; and the theories we can make are relatively simple to analyze. Given a simple theory, it is not hard to make it complicated. The trick is to make a theory that is simple enough to be understood, and valid enough to be a representation of some part of a complicated world.

Beginners in macroeconomics usually have trouble relating the contents of any theory to their direct experience of the world. The theories are neat and abstract, while life is messy and concrete. A brief discussion of the macroeconomic point of view may help meet this difficulty.

Our statements about households (families) relate to what families do with their incomes and the forms in which they keep their wealth. For any individual family, life consists of a series of unexpected expenses and occasional windfall opportunities. As the heads of families grow older, their earning power increases until they reach the age of 45–50 (depending on their occupation) and then declines. Wives take jobs from time to time, depending on the age of their children and their financial needs. In any group of families, we see some that are rising in the social scale and others falling. It would be a monumental task to try to trace the financial history of even a small group of families, let alone a nation, if we considered each family separately.

Some of the events that complicate life for individual families cancel each other out where groups are concerned. While some individuals get sick and have high medical bills, other individuals get well and no longer have such bills. While some individuals get old and retire, others leave childhood, and become self-supporting. While some people decide to buy a car this year, others decide not to buy a car this year. Most of the major unusual events in the lives of individuals are commonplace events in any large group. Graduation from college is a unique event in anyone's life, but colleges every June witness the graduation of whole groups of seniors. Nobody likes to admit it, but one graduating class is, in important respects, "very much like" every other one, taken collectively.

What might be a macroeconomic event that college students might directly observe? One such event occurs every summer, when students are looking for part-time jobs. It is true that most such jobs are obtained after some sort of interview. The individual job applicant knows that he is more likely to get a job if his appearance is neat and if his manners are good. His fate also depends on whether the personnel man he talks to is in a good mood, and happens to like the applicant. But it is a fact that some summers even uncouth students can easily find jobs and that other summers even the "most likely to succeed" types have trouble getting jobs. The difference is not ascribable to the personality of students and personnel men as a group, or to chance, but rather to differences in something called "business conditions." These differences are something that are quite tangible to job applicants, even if they may be difficult to describe precisely.

Most of us have acquaintances or relatives in business organizations. When we ask what they do, it turns out that they spend their time talking to people, making telephone calls, writing letters, and so on. Some of the people involved are more able than others. We all have preferences as to the businesses we deal with—some stores have better goods and better manners than others. We know by reputation the names of some of the most successful business organizations, and we may actually have seen businesses close down in our neighborhoods. Individual businesses, like individual people, vary enormously, and some are much more successful than others.

Imagine, now, that at the end of the year, we could interview all the businesses, and ask them, "Did you sell more this year than last year? Did you earn more profit this year than last year?" and so forth. If the fate of the business depended solely on the personalities of the people who ran it, we should expect to find about as many increases as decreases in sales, and about as many increases as decreases in profits.

As a matter of fact, the results of such surveys are quite different. Some years, most businesses increase their sales and their profits; other years, most businesses have reduced sales and profits. We cannot attribute this fact to personality; businessmen are probably as smart and as aggressive one year as the next.

An impressive list of such visible macroeconomic changes in conditions can be compiled. We know that some years almost all prices rise, and in other years almost all prices fall. We cannot explain this sort of change in terms of individual behavior, and economists therefore seek a systematic way of accounting for the various changes in economic conditions which regularly sweep over entire countries.

These changes must be changes in group behavior and not in individual behavior. When we try to explain macroeconomic events in terms appropriate to individuals, we inevitably encounter the problem: Granted that one individual decides to act differently this year, why isn't his decision offset by someone else, who decides to make the opposite change?

The macroeconomist, in trying to account for the behavior of large groups of people or businesses, asks the question, "What would the world be like if people, as a group, followed certain rules of behavior?" The rules he tries out are obtained in a variety of ways: from intuition, from opinion surveys, from historical observation, and so on. They are usually very simple rules. The macroeconomist does not ordinarily assert that people never deviate from these rules, but he does try to determine what life would be like if the rules were consistently adhered to.

Thus, there are two reasons why it is difficult for beginners to relate the methods of macroeconomics to ordinary direct experience. First, we ordinarily come into direct contact only with individuals, and the notion of "group behavior" is an abstraction which is only partly satisfactory. Second, we are accustomed to so much variation in the behavior of people we know that it is difficult to realize the extent to which this variation is canceled out in large groups of people. These two concessions must be made, however, if we are to arrive at any understanding of the kinds of events which are the subject of our discussion.

Macroeconomic analysis, then, is a logical analysis of how the income and wealth of a community would change if people's behavior were of certain rigidly defined kinds. The macroeconomist is free to analyze any sort of hypothetical behavior he can imagine, but naturally he wants mainly to account for the way people in his own community behave. For this reason, his statements about behavior seek to be at least plausible. On the other hand, they are artificial, at least in the sense of being extremely clean-cut and abstract. We are all tempted to say, in looking at the formulation of an asserted pattern of behavior, "Gee, whiz, people do not follow any rule *that* precisely." To this objection, the macroeconomist can only retort, "Gee, whiz yourself. If you want me to investigate what will happen if people act every which way, all I can say is that anything might happen. That is no way to understand what is going on in the world. As a matter of fact, people do not behave every which way, even if they are a bit erratic sometimes."

Macroeconomics deals with the *total* income and output of the community, the *total* amount of bank deposits, *total* government spending and tax collections, and other variables of this sort. These variables are basically numbers. Some of these are numbers of dollars, some are quantities such as total number of jobs. Therefore, a macroeconomic theory explains what some collection of numbers will turn out to be, given stated conditions. This branch of economics is therefore inherently related to mathematics. It is impossible to discuss macroeconomics in a purely verbal way, because it tries to explain numbers.

A theory is an explanation of the values of certain *variables*. We might decide to make a theory about the interest rate on government bonds and the quantity of paper money in circulation (for example). At any moment, the interest rate is a number and the quantity of paper money in circulation is a number, but from one moment to the next these numbers may change. That is why we refer to them as *variables*. We shall denote the set of variables in a theory by $(V_1, V_2, \cdots, V_n)$, where the subscripts $1, 2, \cdots, n$ stand for the names of the variables. At any moment, each variable has a value, so that the set of variables is momentarily a set of numbers $(\overline{V}_1, \overline{V}_2, \cdots, \overline{V}_n)$.

A theory says that the variables take on particular numerical values because of the operation of some set of *factors*, which we denote by $(F_1, F_2, \cdots, F_m)$. The factors, like the variables, assume particular values at particular moments, and when they do, the factors become a set of numbers, say $(\overline{F}_1, \overline{F}_2, \cdots, \overline{F}_m)$. If a theory has been made correctly, two things can be calculated:

(a) If a particular set of numbers $(\overline{F}_1 \cdots \overline{F}_m)$ is given (so that the factors in the theory assume particular values), then there is a single value that each of the variables may assume. That is,

the set $(\overline{F}_1 \cdots \overline{F}_m)$ *implies a particular set* $(\overline{V}_1 \cdots \overline{F}_n)$

(b) Suppose that in some period, the values of the factors change from $(\bar{F}_1 \cdots \bar{F}_m)$ to $(\hat{F}_1 \cdots \hat{F}_m)$. There will then be a change of ΔF_1 in factor 1, ΔF_2 in factor 2, and so on. Then there is a single set of *changes* that will take place in the variables. That is,

the set $(\Delta F_1 \cdots \Delta F_m)$ *implies a particular set* $(\Delta V_1 \cdots \Delta V_n)$

Another way of putting these statements is that a theory involves a *mapping* of sets $(\bar{F}_1 \cdots \bar{F}_m)$ into sets $(\bar{V}_1 \cdots \bar{V}_n)$ and a *mapping* of sets $(\Delta F_1 \cdots \Delta F_m)$ into sets $(\Delta V_1 \cdots \Delta V_n)$. In general, these two mappings are not the same. There does exist a class of theory for which these two mappings are the same. Such theories are called *linear.* This book is concerned only with linear theories, because these theories are the simplest to analyze, and are thus most suited to beginners.

In order to construct a theory, we assume that *economic units* (consumers, businesses, banks, and government) behave according to clearly defined rules, and we investigate the consequences of their behavior. We are free to assume any rules we like, but in this book, the rules assumed are those which have seemed plausible to several considerable groups of economists. These groups have reached rather different conclusions about how the economy works, and we are able to see why they differ by putting the theories side by side.

It will turn out that when we write down precisely what rules of behavior economic units follow, we obtain a set of statements that can be interpreted as a mapping. That is, when we assume the behavior of economic units depends on variables $(V_1 \cdots V_n)$, and on factors $(F_1 \cdots F_m)$ in a specified way, we are able to say that when the variables take on the particular values, $(\bar{V}_1 \cdots \bar{V}_n)$, then

the set $(\bar{V}_1 \cdots \bar{V}_n)$ *implies a particular set* $(\bar{F}_1 \cdots \bar{F}_m)$

and moreover, if the variables change by amounts $(\Delta V_1 \cdots \Delta V_n)$

the set $(\Delta V_1 \cdots \Delta V_n)$ *implies a particular set* $(\Delta F_1 \cdots \Delta F_m)$

Of course, these behavioral statements are also mappings, but they are "backward." Instead of saying

$(\bar{F}_1 \cdots \bar{F}_m)$ *implies* $(\bar{V}_1 \cdots \bar{V}_n)$

the behavioral statements say

$(\bar{V}_1 \cdots \bar{V}_n)$ *implies* $(\bar{F}_1 \cdots \bar{F}_m)$

Consequently, we must rewrite the behavioral statements so as to obtain other statements that are suitable for our needs. This rewriting is known as *inversion.* In the particular case where all theories are linear, inversion can be accomplished by following a well-defined (although rather boring) sequence of algebraic calculations.

The theories in this book are linear theories, and constructed according to standard rules.

(a) We select a set of variables, whose numerical values we seek to explain in terms of numerical values of some particular set of factors.

(b) We assume that the economic units figuring in our theory follow specified rules of behavior. Then we verify that we have mapped the variables into the factors.

(c) We try to perform an algebraic operation called inversion on the statements in (b). If successful, we have constructed a mapping of the factors into the variables. If unsuccessful, we know that our theory is incomplete or internally inconsistent.

(d) By examining the inverse mapping, we are able to say how each of the factors affects each of the variables in the system.

By insisting that all theories be linear, this book makes it possible for beginners to investigate a wide variety of topics, for all topics are treated according to the same set of rules. This procedure, of course, is justified only as a first step in the direction of understanding economic problems. In research, and even in more advanced courses, the requirement that all theories be linear would be burdensome. That is why advanced work is more difficult than beginning work in economics, as in any field of study.[1]

One particular feature of linear theories is that they must involve "one-to-one mappings" if step (c) is to be undertaken. That is, for any set $(\bar{V}_1 \cdots \bar{V}_n)$, there exists exactly one set $(\bar{F}_1 \cdots \bar{F}_m)$ which can have "caused it," and for any set $(\bar{F}_1 \cdots \bar{F}_m)$, there exists exactly one set $(\bar{V}_1 \cdots \bar{V}_n)$.

Take a simple hypothetical theory in which it is alleged that the number of dollars spent by consumers (denoted by C) in a given year and the interest rate on United States government bonds (denoted by R) depend in a one-to-one way upon two factors: the number of inches of rainfall (denoted by I) and the number of games won by the New York Mets (denoted by G). In constructing the theory we have a one-to-one mapping:

$$(I, G) \xleftrightarrow{\text{Theory}} (C, R)$$

and in particular, suppose that in 1968 it is the case that

$$I = \bar{I}$$

$$G = \bar{G}$$

[1] In more advanced work where nonlinear theories are used, the calculus is necessary rather than simple algebra. In particular, step (c) is very much more difficult. If the calculus is used, however, steps (c) and (d) are replaced by the following:

Step (c′). Show that if the variables change by small enough amounts, then it is possible to construct a linear mapping of *changes* in variables into *changes* in factors. (This is called *differentiation*.) Use the rules of step (c) to perform an algebraic inversion which gives a linear mapping of changes in factors into changes in variables.

Step (d′). Now go back from the mappings of changes to a system in which factors are mapped into variables. [This is called *integration* of the results of step (c′).]

$$C = \bar{C}$$
$$R = \bar{R}$$

are all known. Now, in 1969, rainfall increases from $\bar{R}$ to $(\bar{R} + \Delta R)$. Suppose the Mets win exactly as many games in 1969 as in 1968. Then in 1969, we would have

$$I = \bar{I} + \Delta I$$
$$G = \bar{G}$$
$$C = \bar{C} + \Delta C$$
$$R = \bar{R} + \Delta R$$

But we might ask: Is there any number of games $\hat{G}$ which the Mets *might* have won, such that

$$I = \bar{I} + \Delta I$$
$$G = \hat{G}$$
$$C = \bar{C}$$
$$R = \bar{R}$$

If the theory is one-to-one, the answer to this question is "no." It might be that $C = \bar{C}$ *or* that $R = \bar{R}$ for some value $\hat{G}$, but *never both* $C = \bar{C}$ and $R = \bar{R}$ unless $\Delta I = 0$ and $G = \hat{G}$.

This example is not (in all likelihood) a good economic theory. It does pave the way for a general remark. The United States economy has been characterized by alternate periods of unemployment and of price increases.[2] These have been ascribed by economists as due mainly (except in wartime) to changes in business spending (which we shall call *investment*) on new plant and equipment. One may ask whether it *would be possible* for government to vary its spending in such a way as exactly to offset the effects of variations in business spending on the economy. To this question, theories of the kind presented here would necessarily answer "no." It might be that the government might exactly offset the effects of changes in business spending on *some* parts of the economy. There would necessarily be at least one sector of the economy which is affected differently by business and by government spending. *Some* economists would reject this particular conclusion; *all* economists can probably think of some conclusion they have reached which would be invalid if only one-to-one mappings had theoretical validity. Therefore, it is important for readers to remember that the insistence on one-to-one mappings is a device used to make theories simpler for beginners.

This book is for use in a beginning course, and it therefore is constructed as simply as possible. The price of simplicity, of course, is a loss of variety

[2] Unemployment has never in the past hundred years been as severe as in the 1930s nor price rises as great as in the 1940s, of course.

in the forms of behavior which can be analyzed. To compensate for this loss of variety, there is an important offsetting gain: We may use a standard approach, and a systematic method of analysis to deal with a considerable range of topics. The approach and method are, moreover, closely related to those which are in fact used in more advanced work, so that readers who become used to this method of work will be able to adapt it readily to other methods.

A theory is inherently a simplification. It is an attempt to subject a very complicated reality to a set of rules. If the theory does not match reality in important respects, it should be discarded. It should not be discarded merely because it is simple. The great appeal of macroeconomics is that it suggests simple ways of looking at a few large "pieces" of the economy. The theories given here may be *too* simple; it is not easy, however, to understand the process of reasoning known as theorizing unless one learns it by first considering the simplest examples. In these examples, we consider parts of the economy, taken separately, and we learn how to fit them together.

2

SOCIAL ACCOUNTS AND THEORETICAL DEFINITIONS

This book deals with two subjects, income and wealth, and it explains the connection between them. The income and wealth discussed are those of a country as a whole. A country is an abstraction, and its income and wealth are abstractions. However, a country is also a collection of people to whom income and wealth may be quite tangible. We shall start by considering one part, a person, and move from him to the whole.

It is not obvious that there is a connection between the amount of the income and the amount of the wealth of any individual. If I have inherited $10 million in cash and 10,000 acres of land, I might be considered wealthy. But if I sew my cash into my mattress, leave my land idle, and spend my days watching land and mattress, then I may have no income at all. On the other hand, suppose I earn $1 million a year at my job. If I spend all this income at racetracks and nightclubs, I may own nothing but the shirt on my back. Both of these forms of behavior might be foolish, or unconventional, but both are quite possible. As a matter of fact, the larger a person's income is, the larger I would expect his wealth to be; and the greater his wealth, the larger I would expect his income to be. This statement asserts that out of a variety of possible ways of acting, people, on the average, choose one particular form. The logical connection (if any) between income and wealth, however, is not made clear simply by observing what most people do. It requires a special examination to make this connection clear.

Somewhat the same situation exists about the income and wealth of nations as about those of individual people. The natural wealth of countries like

Brazil and India exceeds that of countries like Japan and Britain, but it is undeveloped. Consequently the income of the first pair is low and that of the second pair is high. But generally we expect wealthy countries (like the United States) to have high incomes and poor countries (like Portugal or Greece) to have low incomes.

Neither the income nor the wealth of a particular country stays the same, and the relative situations of countries change greatly over time. Constantinople (now Istambul) was the wealthiest city west of India in the Middle Ages. The Spaniards who conquered Mexico City found it wealthier than Rome or Constantinople. Marco Polo wondered at the wealth of China, and Vasco da Gama at the wealth of India. Yet Turkey, Mexico, China, and India are now poor countries—they are quite probably poorer than they were five hundred years ago.

Consequently, it is a natural question to ask why the wealth or the income of a country may change. Both of these would be measures of a country's well-being, if we knew what they were. To answer a question such as that just proposed, we go through three steps: (1) We define what we are talking about; (2) we propose an answer; (3) we see whether the answer is the right one. In this chapter, we shall define what we are talking about. In the other chapters we propose answers to the question "Why do a country's income and wealth change?" By placing both income and wealth in a single question, we imply that the two "belong together" in some way as yet unspecified.

In scientific endeavor, part of the task is to learn what questions can be usefully answered. The general question in the last paragraph, "Why do a country's income and wealth change?" is too vague to be of much use. In any theory, one proposes smaller, sharper, more specific questions. Thus a theory in this book proposes questions such as, "What will happen to consumer spending if the quantity of money in the economy changes?" or "What will happen to the amount of government tax revenue if business investment changes?" The questions asked are answered within the framework of a theory. If the conditions assumed do not hold, the answer is not valid. Theorists are able to give several possible answers to a question because they are able to construct several possible patterns of economic behavior.

Readers may wonder why one should advance several answers to a question—presumably only one of these is the right answer. But there is usually no single, right answer to this kind of question; only varying degrees of error. Economists, therefore, are usually in the position of trying to improve on an answer that has some good points and some bad points. Proposing answers, then, is a necessary and recognized part of economics. It is called *theorizing*, and a theory is a proposed answer to some question. It requires special training to be able even to propose an answer. It requires special training, of a different sort, to decide whether a proposal is acceptable. This book is a "how-to-do-it" book. It tells you how to propose a serious answer to a serious question.

In this book, we divide the community into four kinds of economic units: households, businesses (other than banks), banks, and government. We consider all units of any kind together, in a lump. In this chapter, we tell how to "lump" together economic units. In order to explain this procedure, we first explain the things that must be combined.

The activities of an economic unit are described by the records it keeps. For present purposes, these records are called *accounts*. There are two basic sets of accounts. The first, called the *balance sheet*, describes what the economic unit had at some moment, and how it got it. The second, called the *income statement*, describes what the business did, in some period of time.

Although businesses usually keep reasonably complete records, households do not. Nevertheless, it is convenient to talk as if all economic units kept good records. On this basis, the total wealth and the total income of a community consist of the sum of the wealth and of the income of all the economic units in the community. The process of adding up individual sets of accounts gives a set of *social accounts*. Some countries have reasonably complete and accurate statistics for many of the social accounts. Others do not. But it is convenient to talk about social accounts as if all the data required could actually be collected. If they could be, then proposed explanations of changes in income and wealth could be tested.

The explanations advanced here will be kept as simple as possible. That is, they omit certain details on the grounds that they are unimportant. Skeptical readers will ask themselves whether the omissions are really unimportant. To make this decision, they must determine whether the detail in question matters for the purpose at hand.

Let us consider an example. Mr. A buys a house from Mr. B for $20,000. A simple way of describing this transaction would be: Before the transaction Mr. A had $20,000 in cash, Mr. B had a house. After the transaction, Mr. B had $20,000 and Mr. A had a house. Actually, this description may omit a number of complicating details, because:

(1) Mr. B paid a commission to a real-estate agent for finding a buyer
(2) Mr. A paid a lawyer to examine the title—if Mr. B did not have legal title to the house, he could not deliver it to Mr. A
(3) if Mr. B sold the house for more than he paid for it, he may become liable to a capital gains tax to the Federal Government, and perhaps a second tax to his state government
(4) the bill of sale allocated property taxes currently due on the house between Mr. A and Mr. B
(5) Mr. A registered his title to the house with an appropriate local govern-

ment agency, so that his claim to ownership will be recognized; he paid a fee for this registration.

Do these various miscellaneous operations, undertaken in the course of transaction, matter enough to be itemized? The answer is, "That depends." For Mr. A and Mr. B they matter, because the various lawyers, real-estate agents, and tax officials will insist on being paid. If Mr. B has borrowed money (got a mortgage) on his house, he will have to show the lender that he has acquired the house with the money he borrowed; if Mr. A had borrowed money (got a mortgage) when he originally bought the house, he will have to pay off his debt from the proceeds of the sale. In analyzing the operations of the market for real estate, one would have to take into account all the various business and government interests which take part in the operation. But even so, if the side payments made are relatively small compared to the basic $20,000, and if they do not have much effect on either Mr. A's or Mr. B's decisions about the transaction, we can retain the simple description given above: The sale of a standing house basically involves the transfer of $20,000 in cash from buyer to seller, and of a house from seller to buyer. The side payments are "mere complications," although they may be an important aspect of daily life to real-estate firms, lawyers, and tax-collecting agencies.

This example also brings out the difference between business accounting and social accounting. Mr. A gave up cash and received a house. Mr. B gave up a house and received cash. One event is described by four bookkeeping entries. Two of these are in Mr. A's books, and two are in Mr. B's books. Business or "double-entry" accounting takes into consideration the fact that there was an exchange of money for a house. Social accounting recognizes that more than one set of accounts is involved in any transaction, and social accounting may be thought of as "quadruple-entry" accounting. Business accountants will not be worried by the fact that both Mr. A and Mr. B have a record of the sale of the house. Social accountants must worry about this fact. Suppose they forget it, and then try to count how many houses changed hands during the year. Then they will count the house once when they look at Mr. A's records, and a second time when they look at Mr. B's records. Thus social accounting involves problems which do not concern business accountants. But social accountants start from the same set of records as business accountants.

The next step is to describe the accounting data on which the later discussion rests. There follow short descriptions of balance sheets, income statements, the relation between balance sheets and income statements, and the "addition" process which combines the accounts of individual economic units into social accounts.

BALANCE SHEETS

The balance sheet of an economic unit lists the values of things owned by the unit, and the way in which funds were acquired to buy these things. Although any economic unit may be considered as having a balance sheet, it is simplest to discuss the balance sheets of businesses in detail, making some comparisons with other balance sheets as needed.

Things owned by a business are called *assets*, and the list of assets, and their valuations, make up the *asset side* of the balance sheet. A complete discussion of how values are placed on these assets is beyond the scope of this book. Particular attention will be paid to the following assets:

(1) *Cash* mainly consists of checking accounts in banks. Smaller amounts consist of paper money and coin.
(2) *Accounts receivable* are sums owed to the business by its customers.
(3) *Securities* consist of stocks and bonds issued by *other* economic units. (The securities issued by an economic unit are discussed below.) These represent claims that the business has on other businesses (and government), and they are a source of income to the business.
(4) *Inventories* consist of raw materials, partly finished and finished goods that are owned by the business.
(5) *Plant and equipment* consists of land, buildings, and machinery owned by the business.

Naturally, the composition of the assets of different kinds of economic units varies. Electric generating companies' assets consist mainly of plant. Financial institutions such as banks have almost no assets other than cash and securities. (To be exact, "loans" made directly to individual customers, securities bought in the mortgage and corporate and government bond markets, and cash are the main assets.) For families, inventories are small, and houses make up most of the item corresponding to "plant and equipment." For companies in retail trade, accounts receivable are a large item, because consumer credit is an important aspect of doing business with the public. Some of these differences may be important in our later work. For the moment, it is enough to note that they exist.

The balance sheet contains a second list, called the *liabilities side*, which divides assets according to the ways in which their purchase was financed: They were purchased either on credit, or from contributions made by the owners of the business, or from profits of the business. These three categories contain all logical possibilities, so that the total of the liabilities side necessarily equals the total assets.

The fact that total assets equal total liabilities does not mean, of course, that we can necessarily identify how the purchase of individual assets of a business was financed. In some cases such association is possible. Suppose that the business (or family) bought land and buildings and obtained a *mortgage* loan to pay for them. Then the lender has a claim on that particular group of assets. Ordinarily there is no such direct association between particular assets and particular items on the liabilities side of the balance sheet.

The debt of a business consists of *accounts payable*, which may be thought of as charge accounts owed by the business; of *loans* by banks and other financial institutions, made usually for periods of less than two years; and of *bonds*. Bonds are certificates ordinarily representing long-term debts (ten to thirty years). The company issuing the bonds guarantees repayment and interest to any legal owner. Consequently, bonds may be bought and sold and the composition of the creditors owning the bonds may change. (The creditor who makes a loan cannot sell the "IOU" to anyone else in any simple way.)[1]

The contribution of owners to the business is called *capital stock*, and certificates are issued by the business to owners in proportion to their contribution. This capital stock is not a debt of the business. The owners of stock are not guaranteed any fixed return, but they have a claim on the earnings of the business.

Finally, if the profits of the business are kept in the business, an *earned surplus* account appears on the liabilities side of the balance sheet.

Stocks and bonds are quite different kinds of securities from a legal point of view. The income that stock owners receive is called *dividends*, and is different from the *interest* earned by bondholders. It usually varies with the profits earned by the business, while interest payments are fixed. There is more opportunity for gain, and also more risk of loss to stockholders.

In coming chapters, in the interests of simplification, we shall usually treat all securities as if they were bonds. This practice is followed in part to hold down the number of things that must be kept track of, thereby simplifying the work. This combining of stocks and bonds under the heading "bonds" is also justified by the fact that securities are looked at mainly from the point of view of investors seeking a return in the form of income. Some investors, of course, buy stocks in order to obtain a share in the management of the business—one of the rights of stockholders. But in large corporations, most stockholders have no aspirations to a share in management, and are only concerned with a return on an investment. In this respect, they are not unlike bondholders.

[1] Most people think of bonds in terms of the savings bonds issued by the U.S. Government. These may not be bought and sold. On the other hand, they may be redeemed at fixed prices, whereas the price of "marketable" bonds varies from day to day with market conditions.

Thus, the liabilities side of a balance sheet is composed of:

(1) Accounts payable
(2) Direct borrowings (loans)
(3) Securities issued
  (a) Bonds
  (b) Stocks
(4) Earned surplus

The relative importance of these accounts varies with different kinds of economic units. Electric power companies' liabilities accounts consist mainly of bonds, although stocks and earned surplus make up most of the liabilities side of other nonbank businesses. The deposits made by customers make up almost all of the liabilities side of bank balance sheets—because the bank owes these sums to its depositors, and agrees to repay them at once (in the case of checking accounts) or in a month or two (in the case of savings accounts), if the depositors wish.

Nobody "owns" a family but its members, so that the item "stocks" has no exact meaning. Also, families do not make profit, so that "earned surplus" has no exact meaning. But the term *net worth* is sometimes used to represent the difference between what a family owns and its debts. (This same term, net worth, also is used to denote the sum of capital stock and earned surplus in business accounts.)

It is common practice to designate balance sheets by what is called a T-diagram. For example, the T-diagram that has been described above would have the following format:

Assets	*Liabilities*
Cash	Accounts payable
Accounts receivable	Loans
Securities	Bonds
Inventories	Stock
Plant and equipment	Earned surplus

Of course, the balance sheets of firms, and the balance sheets used in theories, have numbers entered in the individual accounts. In formulating particular theories, of course, it will turn out to be useful to suppress even this amount of detail. In the next chapter, for instance, the following very simple balance sheet will appear:

Cash, M	Net worth, W
Plant and equipment, K	

Here, of course, most of the accounts have been suppressed, because a *very* simple theory is discussed. The symbols M, K, and W stand for variables. The purpose of the theory is to find out what numerical value each variable will have under certain conditions.

INCOME STATEMENTS

Income is received as a payment for goods produced or services rendered. Not all money received represents income. If I borrow from a bank, I receive money, but I do not receive income. If I sell an asset, such as a house or a car, I am also paid money, but this money is not income. Moreover, not all income is in the form of money. Thus, farm labor (and college students) sometimes get paid room and board for their labor; businesses sell on credit and have income in the form of "accounts receivable," and so on.

To know whether an item represents income, we must have a definition of the activity of the economic unit in question. A builder who sells a house that he has built receives income. If a family sells its house, it sells an asset and does not receive income. A statement of this sort depends on a way of recognizing house builders, and distinguishes between them and others. The example just given is fairly clear; other examples might be harder to sort out.

The *income statement* records the income of an economic unit and the uses to which it is put. We shall discuss the income statements of businesses in detail and then make some brief comparisons of such statements with the income statements of households.

The income statement completely accounts for the income received. Thus, by definition, for a business, income equals cost plus profit. The total calculation runs as follows:

Income equals the sum of
- *Cost*, consisting of
  - variable cost
    - materials, supplies, and others
    - labor
  - fixed cost
    - depreciation
    - rent
    - interest
    - taxes, other than profits taxes
- *Profit*, divided into
  - taxes on profit
  - dividends paid to stockholders
  - retained profits

The terms *variable cost* and *fixed cost* are based on the following principle: Some costs depend on the level of a firm's output, while others do not. A firm can vary its labor costs by hiring workers or laying off workers; it can vary its materials costs by buying larger or smaller amounts from suppliers. But other costs do not vary with output. The interest payments of a business, for instance, depend on its borrowings not on its output. Interest payments can, of course, be altered if the firm is able to borrow or to repay its debts and if interest rates change. Thus the term "fixed" is defined only with reference to changes in output.

To some extent, the measurement of any of these quantities is artificial. A large firm buying from many suppliers and having large inventories of materials on hand may find it hard to tell exactly how much of its purchases was actually used in manufacturing finished goods, and how much was put into storage.

Depreciation, however, is the largest single element of uncertainty in the income statement. Depreciation measures the wearing out of plant and equipment owned by the firm. This wearing out is a cost to the business. If depreciation is not counted as a cost in the accounts, the business will estimate its profits as being higher than if depreciation is counted. If these higher profits are then paid out as taxes or dividends, then when the plant and equipment are no longer usable, the business will have to raise outside funds to replace them; it may in fact be unable to do so because this practice is considered a sign of very bad management. Depreciation is an *imputation*: The business does not pay this cost to anyone else. Instead, it charges a special account, which is akin to retained earnings in generating funds from inside the business. Accountants call the sum of profits and depreciation the *cash flow*, since both can be a source of funds that can be used to pay for expansion of the business.

In the discussion of balance sheets it was stated that for many investors, interest and dividends were similar in principle, differing only in detail. From the point of view of management, dividends and interest both represent payments of income to outsiders; hence both reduce the amount of money that the firm can retain to help finance its growth. In this sense, "cash flow" terminology corresponds to the economic view used in the present discussion.

The income statement of households is different from that of businesses in several respects. Thus "costs" of a family represent its current spending on goods and services. The family has no owner, and therefore there are no "dividends," all "profit" being retained. But profit is simply that part of income that is not part of "cost." For a family, therefore, if "cost" is associated with current spending, "profit" must be associated with savings.

The statement in the preceding paragraph is an attempt at reconciling business and family accounting methods. It is important to remember that this reconciliation can never be perfect because families, after all, are unlike businesses. Nevertheless, to the extent that there is some similarity between the two kinds of accounts, it is natural to emphasize it. This similarity encourages us to treat income of families and of businesses in a similar spirit, and it gives us a framework within which we can speak of a basic similarity of things that superficially are rather different.

THE RELATION BETWEEN BALANCE SHEET AND INCOME STATEMENTS

Thus far, balance sheets and income statements have been treated as quite distinct. Physically speaking, they are listed separately in the annual report of a business. On the other hand, there is a close relation between the two. This relation is described by saying that *changes in balance sheet accounts may be associated with elements in income statements.*

A very simple illustration of this principle is the case of depreciation. Depreciation is an item of cost. It measures the amount of wearing out of plant and equipment. If depreciation takes place, the value of plant and equipment owned by the business decreases. Therefore, if a business does not buy any new plant, the *change* in the value of its plant during the course of a year should be the same as the cost item, depreciation.

Let us now consider a very condensed form of a balance sheet:

Assets	*Liabilities*
Cash (including accounts receivable)	Inside funds (earned surplus and accumulated depreciation)
Earning assets (all other assets)	Outside funds (debt plus capital stock)
Total	Total

This way of combining balance sheet accounts has the following rationale:

(1) Securities are owned by the firm, because they yield a return. Plant, equipment, and inventory are all held because the business uses them to make its output, and hence to make profits. In this sense they are different from cash and accounts receivables, which do not yield a return.

(2) Inside funds represent income earned and kept in the business. Outside funds are obtained by borrowing and from the owner's contribution to the business (capital stock).

This classification of the balance sheet also gives a tidy way of relating income accounts to changes in balance sheets.

(3) Saving consists of that part of a family's income which is not spent on goods and services. It consists of that part of a business's income which is not paid out to others in the form of costs or taxes or dividends. That is, savings represents an increase in the net worth of an economic unit over some period of time.
(4) Investment consists in the purchase of income-earning assets by an economic unit during some period of time.

Savings may be used to pay off debt. If they are not so used, they may be kept in the form of increased cash balances, or they may be invested. Thus, for any individual, some savings may be invested.

Investments may be paid for in a variety of ways. The economic unit may simply reduce its cash balance to pay for the investment; or it may borrow to pay for the investment; or it may pay for the investment out of savings.

No two concepts have caused macroeconomists more trouble than the concepts of savings and investment. This book refers only occasionally to savings. It is worth considering just why this practice is followed, for it may annoy some readers. Savings are necessarily defined in a negative way:

(1) Economic units save when they fail to spend part of their income.
(2) Economic units save when they invest, provided they fail to reduce their cash balances and also fail to increase their debts.

To measure savings, we proceed in one of two ways. We may define certain actions which we say constitute "spending one's income," and obtain savings by subtracting this spending from total income. We may also define certain assets which we consider to be "cash" (or at any rate nonincome-producing). Then we take the total increase in assets, subtract from it the increase in debt, and the remainder will be savings. For any individual, the two procedures yield the same results. But for the economy as a whole, the two methods use statistics that are generated in different ways, and there are important practical problems in reconciling the two methods of calculating.

In preparing theories such as those used in this book, we make suggestions as to how people behave. It is easier to say how people behave than how they fail to behave. Thus if economic behavior consists of buying consumer goods, buying plant, buying securities, holding cash, and borrowing, we may have to assign a rule to people's behavior with regard to each activity. From these rules we may deduce a rule about their savings. It would, of course, be possible to assume rules about buying consumer goods, buying plant, buying securities, holding cash, and saving, and from these deduce a rule about borrowing. But this alternative procedure seems to make for more difficult theories. As a matter of convenience, then, we find it easier to leave savings as a variable which may (if the reader wishes) be derived from the rest of the system.

It is important for readers to remember that in a theory, concepts such as investment, savings, and consumption are defined by the requirements of logic and consistency alone. When it comes to applying theories to the real world, economists must provide a clear reason for associating a theoretical term with some set of observable actions.

For example, consumption (in theory) consists of the purchase of goods and services. If a family buys a package of soft drinks and drinks them, it is consuming. If the family stores them on the shelf, it is adding to inventory and hence investing. What if the family buys a refrigerator? A car? A house? A suit of clothes? Our rule for deciding whether these purchases are consumption is: Do they provide income? (If they provide income, they are earning assets and, hence, investment.) But houses may be rented by their owners; many people need cars for business purposes; and even a suit of clothes may be bought to impress a customer. Consequently, in applying our rule, the social accountant will have to make great numbers of detailed decisions and guesses in order to provide information in a form that is relevant to the behavior rules proposed by a theory.

The detailed matching of accounting procedures to theoretical specifications is a subject in itself, and is dealt with in another volume of this series. It is treated in a superficial way in this book, which shows how to construct simple theories about income and wealth. The work of economists does not end when theories have been proposed, but it cannot properly be begun without such proposals.

The question of depreciation is one that usually causes trouble for beginners. Depreciation is a cost item in the income statement of a business. It is not, however, a cost paid to anyone outside the business. In this respect, it is an imputation. It is income that is not spent. It is, in this sense savings, and an addition to net worth.

But the depreciation account stands for the wearing out of plant in the production process. As the plant wears out, it is presumably worth less. Consequently, if the plant is valued each year, its valuation will fall each year. If the depreciation cost is correctly calculated, it will exactly equal the decline in the value of the plant. Therefore, the business may keep its books in one of two equivalent ways:

On a *gross* basis, the change in total assets due to investment is given by:

$$\text{Additions to plant} = \text{New plant purchased}$$

which equals

$$\text{Additions to the liabilities side of the balance sheet} = \text{New borrowings plus depreciation charges}$$

On a *net* basis, the change in total assets due to investment is given by:

Additions to plant = New plant purchased, *minus* wearing out of old plant (depreciation)

which equals

Additions to the liabilities side of the balance sheet = New borrowings

Depreciation is an important practical source of funds for business. It represents income that is not paid out and (since most income is in cash) a large flow of cash into the business. On the other hand, it is not a very interesting item, because accounting practice is rather inflexible. Charges to depreciation accounts do not change much from year to year, and they do not add much of interest to the problems talked about later in this book For this reason, most of the discussion will be on a "net basis"—the change in earning assets will be the same thing as investment, and the change in inside funds will be the same as retained profits, that is, savings.

The changes in balance sheets may involve quite a lot of bustle and noise, for the activities of certain kinds of business organizations are mainly concerned with these changes. When banks lend money, they change their assets and the debts of others. When individuals buy or sell in the stock market, they are changing the composition of their assets. When insurance companies invest the premiums they receive, their assets change. When families buy houses, their assets change. Certain kinds of businesses—banking, insurance companies, finance companies, stockbrokers, for instance—are more involved in balance sheet transactions than in income transactions. These, taken collectively, form the *money market*, sometimes also called the *capital market* or *financial markets*. The operations of such companies are of very considerable interest, and one important part of macroeconomics deals with them.

ADDING ECONOMIC UNITS TOGETHER

Adding income statements or balance sheets together is called *aggregation.* The discussion of income and wealth has been confined to individual economic units. It has been shown that there is a natural connection among the various parts of individual balance sheets and income statements. It has also been shown that changes in balance sheets may be related to income statements. These natural connections should be maintained when an aggregation takes place. Unless aggregation is done properly, however, these connections cannot be maintained.

In aggregating balance sheets, there is a problem involving financial instruments. Suppose the following three firms' balance sheets must be added up:

Firm A

Cash,	C_A	Borrowings,	L_A
Earning assets,	E_A	Net worth,	N_A

Firm B

Cash,	C_B	Borrowings,	L_B
Earning assets,	E_B	Net worth,	N_B

Bank

Loans,	$L_A + L_B$	Deposits,	$C_A + C_B$

There is no particular problem about adding A and B together:

A plus B

Cash,	$C_A + C_B$	Borrowings,	$L_A + L_B$
Earning assets,	$E_A + E_B$	Net worth,	$N_A + N_B$

But for the group of three firms, simple addition yields:

A + B + Bank

Cash,	$C_A + C_B$	Deposits,	$C_A + C_B$
Loans,	$L_A + L_B$	Loans,	$L_A + L_B$
Earning assets,	$E_A + E_B$	Net worth,	$N_A + N_B$

For some purposes, we might be tempted to cancel cash and loans from both sides of this balance sheet. The group as a whole owes these sums to itself. From a group point of view, we might argue as follows: Suppose I have a dime in my right-hand pocket. I lend it to my left-hand pocket, and put an IOU into my right-hand pocket. Then do I have 20 cents' assets, a dime, and an IOU? There are many who claim that the balance sheet just set down is a complicated version of this transaction. From some points of view they may be right. If, however, the actions of A and B depend in some meaningful way upon the debts they have incurred, then there is no way of discussing these actions if we talk in terms of a balance sheet which suppresses the loan items. Consequently, there may be cases in which it is very useful to use a balance sheet which shows explicitly that some group owes itself sums of money.

The aggregation problem in income accounting is called the *value-added* problem. It exists because businesses buy from each other. Consider the following example: Coal is used to make steel, and steel is used to make automobiles. The accounts of coal producers list wages, taxes, interest, and profits as offsets to the income obtained from the sale of coal. The accounts of the steel producers list coal, wages, taxes, interest, rent, and profits as offsets to the income obtained from the sale of steel. The accounts of automobile producers list steel, wages, taxes, interest, rent, and profits as offsets to the income obtained from the sale of automobiles. The combined payments of wages, taxes, interest, rent, and profits by these three industries represent the total offsets to their combined income. But if we add together the sales of the three industries, they will exceed these combined payments. This is because the sales of the coal mines figure as a cost of the steel industry, and the sales of the steel mills figure as a cost of the automobile industry.

The guiding principle of income accounting is that all income is earned by producing goods and services, and that all production generates income. But a given act of production generates income only once; that is, for its producer. Consequently, if the sales of industries are added up, double-counting will take place whenever one business buys from another. To obtain a total production figure that avoids double-counting, it is necessary in "adding up" business firms to subtract, from their sales figures, the value of any goods they purchased from other business firms on the grounds that these values have already been counted elsewhere. If such exclusion is made, the value of business sales will indeed equal wages plus taxes, plus interest plus rent, plus profits. The sum of these "factors of production" is then equal to the "value added in manufacture" of businesses.

Arithmetically, this treatment of the value-added problem amounts to an *addition rule.* Let S_A and S_B be the sales of two sets of businesses called A and B. Now let $C = A \cup B$ be the set of all businesses which are either in A or in B. The *value-added rule* states:

$$S_C = S_A + S_B - (S_{AB} + S_{BA})$$

where S_{AB} represents sales by firms in set A to firms in set B, and S_{BA} represents sales by firms in set B to firms in set A.

If this rule is followed, then S_T, where T is the set of all firms in the economy, will equal the income of all other sectors of the community (households, government, banks) plus business savings (that is, retained profits). If this rule is *not* followed, this equality will not hold.

Problem Show that this last assertion is true.

Problem Consider income paid by one household to another for services rendered, such as interest on loans. Can you formulate a rule analogous to the value-added rule to cope with this situation? Can you arrive at an identity like that in the preceding problem?

The national *income*, then, consists of income earned by all businesses, by households, and by government, providing that no particular item is counted more than once. Businesses receive income from other businesses, from households, and from government. That is, they receive a part of the total spending by other businesses, by households, and by government. As a whole, income is earned if and only if goods and services are produced, so that the national income and the national product are the same thing. The national product, of course, consists of goods and services consumed by households and government. It also includes goods and services purchased by business. These business purchases consist of acquisition of the plant and equipment, and the inventories by businesses. Since these purchases add to the earning assets of business, they constitute investment. Thus:

Y (the total national product)
equals C (consumption by households)
plus I (investment by businesses)
plus G (government spending)

TWO REMARKS

(1) We disregard foreign trade in this book. Transactions with foreign countries represent a source of income and also a use of purchasing power. In analyzing countries that depend heavily on foreign trade, such as the European countries, this omission would be an important source of error.
(2) The classification given here is based on the needs of this book. In fact, in part of this book we disregard government, and therefore pretend that $Y = C + I$, with $G = 0$. It would be sensible for many purposes to break up the aggregates listed here. For instance, in the United States, consumer spending on "nondurables" (food, clothing, gasoline, fuel, and rent) is relatively stable, while expenditures on "durables" (furniture, household appliances, and automobiles) is subject to fluctuations of a much greater amplitude and complexity. A detailed analysis of the economy might well require breaking C into parts.

Although the national product is equal to the combined income of households, business, and government, it is difficult to compute the separate components in detail. Strictly speaking, the calculation to be made is:

Y (the total national income)
equals Y_C disposable personal income (household income after taxes)
plus Y_B disposable business income (that is, retained business profits)
plus Y_G tax revenue

Accountants are reluctant to treat retained business profits as "disposable business income" because this treatment would imply that dividends are a cost of production, which is not really the case. But it is not right to include dividends both as business income and also as household income. Also, tax revenue such as sales taxes goes directly to government without ever passing through the income accounts of businesses.

Data on total household income are collected according to the legal form of that income (that is, wages, interest, rent, dividends, and so on). We know how much income households earn, and we know what total personal income taxes are, but we have no way of knowing how much of any given *kind* of personal income is paid out in taxes. The reason is that the federal income tax laws are based on total income from all sources and are not computed separately on each kind of income.

As a result, the usual national income statistics are calculated according to the rule:

Y	(total national income)
equals H	personal income *before* taxes[2]
plus B	business income (total profits, *minus* dividends; or retained profits *plus* profits tax)
plus T	indirect business taxes (that is, tax revenue on sales and excise taxes)[3]

HISTORICAL REMARK

Economists in the eighteenth and early nineteenth centuries were greatly interested in the shares of the national income received by labor, landowners, and money-lenders. Entire theories of economics were developed on the assumption that certain types of service were "productive" and others not. Thus, the eighteenth century French "Physiocratic," and the nineteenth century American "Single Tax" writers held that only land was productive. English economists from Adam Smith to Ricardo held that only labor was productive, and this view is still held by Marxists. These theories are too complicated and too imprecise to be discussed here. But it is easy to see that the classification of income into wages, rent, interest, and dividends would be the same as the determination of the income of "economic classes," providing that each household obtains all its income from a single source. Modern economics concentrates on the utilization of income $(C + I + G)$ rather than on the sources of income.

The first known attempt at computing the national income was made in

[2] This is the sum of wages, interest, rent, and dividends paid to households.

[3] Some economists maintain that these indirect business taxes do not represent a part of the value of output, because government collects these taxes without having contributed to making goods and services. If indirect taxes are subtracted from the gross income and the gross product, a valuation "at factor cost" rather than "at market prices" is obtained.

England, around 1600, by Gregory King. Not until the mid-nineteenth century was the attempt repeated. During the 1920s and early 1930s, a number of current estimates of national income were made for various countries. These estimates were considered at the time to be mere curiosities, albeit of interest to economic historians. In the late 1930s, however, it was realized that such information, if made promptly available, was of great usefulness to government and business in interpreting economic conditions. The change in attitude occurred because theories about short-run changes in the national income were developed. Since 1946, the U.S. Department of Commerce has made quarterly estimates of the national income and product, and has made a steady effort to improve its reporting. This system of accounts owes its present state to the pioneering statistical work of the National Bureau of Economic Research and to the theoretical work of J. M. Keynes.

The portion of the analysis that deals with balance sheets derives from a much older branch of economics—*monetary economics*. Much of it goes back to the time of the Napoleonic Wars, when British wartime inflation and postwar recession brought a major development of economic analysis. In the United States, the development of current banking statistics dates from the establishment of the Federal Reserve System in 1913. Thus, analytical discussion of the banking system has been going on for a long time. The formal attempt to combine income statement and balance sheet analysis stems, in recent years, from empirical work by Morris Copeland, the initiator of the "moneyflows" system of accounts; and from the theoretical work on "financial intermediaries" by Gurley and Shaw.

The statistical work done so far is more complete in its calculations of changes in assets and liabilities than in its reporting of total levels of these accounts. There are great practical difficulties arising in the consolidation of balance sheets maintained on differing accounting principles by different businesses, and by the absence of balance sheet data for households. Even in the banking system, where statistics are much more detailed and complete than in other sectors of the economy, it has only recently become possible to separate business and household bank balances.

One subject that has attracted considerable interest in recent years is the connection between changes in price and changes in quantity. The next four chapters explain in fairly simple ways the connection between incomes and balance sheets. The connection between price and quantity changes in either income or balance sheet accounts remains much more troublesome. Theories that separate these two effects are, in the main, much more difficult than the kind presented here.

However, one feature of any discipline seems to be that problems turn out to be simpler than were originally thought. The theory presented here as Tiny Model 1 was the object of very learned discussion in the 1930s. It did not reach the undergraduate program in any satisfactory form until the first edition of Samuelson's *Economics*, in 1946. It now appears very simple; in this book it is disposed of in a page or two. But it continues to be a building block in more comprehensive theories.

Only the definitive books deal with subjects that are dead because nothing need further be known about them. The subjects discussed here are very much alive. To put it differently, much remains to be learned. The theories presented here are partial theories; none claims to deal with the entire economy. But the careful reader can get exercise in putting together pieces of the economy. In time he will become able to do more realistic, and hence more difficult work.

3

SIMPLE THEORIES

A FIRST EXAMPLE

Tiny Model 1

This chapter presents several very simple theories, and discusses a compact way of writing down and analyzing the more interesting and complicated theories given in the rest of the book. Chapter 2 has presented a social accounting system which defines some of the relations among the income and balance sheet accounts of the community. Every theory discussed here includes some piece of this social accounting system. It also includes some assumptions about how economic units in that piece of the economy act. If the theory has been constructed soundly, it will tell what the values of some interesting variables in the economy will turn out to be, and what may make them change.

Our first example of a theory will be called Tiny Model 1. It is the simplest imaginable theory of the national income, and for this reason it is always taught to beginners. This theory assumes two things to be true:

(1) The national product accounts are as follows:

$$Y = C + I$$

where Y = national product; C = consumption; I = investment.

This statement comes from the definition of the national product in Chapter 2, simplified by disregarding government spending.

(2) Consumer spending depends on income, in the following way:

$$C = aY + F_c$$

a and F_c are constants.

This statement says that whenever the national income (the national product) increases by \$1.00, consumption will increase by \$$a$. This conclusion is valid, because

$$C' = a(Y + 1) + F_c$$
$$C = aY + F_c$$

Subtracting gives the change in consumption ($C' - C$) resulting from the \$1.00 increase in income.

$$C' - C = a$$

The symbol a is called the "marginal propensity to consume" for historical reasons which need not concern us.

If people consume more than their incomes rise, $a > 0$. But they do not consume all of their income. They also save some. Savings has been defined in Chapter 2 as an increase in net worth. The way people increase their net worth is by spending less than they earn. Thus, savings is defined for the present purpose as

$$S = Y - C = Y - aY - F_c$$
$$= (1 - a)Y - F_c$$

If income rises by \$1.00, savings will change by \$$(1 - a)$

$$S' = (1 - a)(Y + 1) - F_c$$
$$S = (1 - a)Y \qquad - F_c$$
$$S' - S = (1 - a)$$

Therefore, if people save more when their income rises, $(1 - a) > 0$. (This will be our assumption.) Therefore, a is greater than zero and less than one.

Tiny Model 1 says that if investment (I), the marginal propensity to consume (a), and autonomous[1] consumption (F_c) are given, consumption and the national product are uniquely determined. To show that this is indeed the case, write

$$Y = C + I$$
$$C = aY + F_c$$

Substituting the second equation in the first,

$$Y = aY + F_c + I$$
$$(1 - a)Y = F_c + I$$
$$Y = \frac{1}{1 - a}F_c + \frac{1}{1 - a}I$$

[1] Consumption is thought of as being in two parts. One part (aY) depends on the national income. It may be called *induced* consumption. The other part (F_c) is called *autonomous* because it does not depend on anything in the system.

Therefore, Y is determined by a, F_c, and I. Now substitute for Y in the second equation:

$$C = a\left(\frac{1}{1-a}F_c + \frac{1}{1-a}I\right) + F_c$$

$$= \left(1 + \frac{a}{1-a}\right)F_c + \frac{a}{1-a}I$$

$$= \frac{1}{1-a}F_c + \frac{a}{1-a}I$$

Thus, C is determined by a, F_C, and I. This shows that if F_C and I are known, we may calculate what C and Y will be. But it does not prove that there is only one possible value of C and only one possible value of Y for any given value of I and F_C.

Imagine that $I = \bar{I}$ and $F_C = \bar{F}_C$ represent fixed levels of investment and autonomous spending. Suppose that there are two amounts of consumption C_1 and C_2 and two levels of national product Y_1 and Y_2 which are compatible with $\bar{I}$ and $\bar{F}_C$. Then

$$\frac{a}{1-a}\bar{I} + \frac{1}{1-a}\bar{F}_C = C_1$$

and

$$\frac{a}{1-a}\bar{I} + \frac{1}{1-a}\bar{F}_C = C_2$$

Subtract the second from the first

$$0 = C_1 - C_2 \quad \text{or} \quad C_1 = C_2$$

Similarly, it can be shown that

$$0 = Y_1 - Y_2 \quad \text{or} \quad Y_1 = Y_2$$

Thus, there is exactly one solution; that is, one value of C and one value of Y for any given values of I and F_C.

Thus, Tiny Model 1 states that if the pair (I, F_C) are known, the pair (Y, C) are uniquely determined. It also says that if the pair (Y, C) are known, the pair (I, F_C) are uniquely determined. Therefore, the theory actually may be thought of in two ways. The first is represented by the pair of equations

$$\begin{aligned} \frac{a}{1-a}I + \frac{1}{1-a}F_C &= C \\ \frac{1}{1-a}I + \frac{1}{1-a}F_C &= Y \end{aligned} \tag{3.1}$$

The second is represented by the pair of equations we started with

$$\begin{aligned} Y - C &= I \\ -aY + C &= F_C \end{aligned} \tag{3.2}$$

There is a reason for considering both ways of writing this theory. One of them is closer to ordinary experience; the other enables us to answer two questions about the economy. The statement $C = aY + F_C$ has an intuitive meaning concerning how consumers act, and it is natural to formulate a statement about consumers in a form such as this. But suppose we wish to find out the consequence on the economy of an increase of one dollar in investment or autonomous consumption. In the first case,

$$\frac{a}{1-a}(I+1) + \frac{1}{1-a}F_C = C_1$$

$$\frac{a}{1-a}I \qquad + \frac{1}{1-a}F_C = C$$

Subtracting,

$$\frac{a}{1-a} \qquad = (C_1 - C)$$

$$\frac{1}{1-a}(I+1) + \frac{1}{1-a}F_C = Y_1$$

$$\frac{1}{1-a}I \qquad + \frac{1}{1-a}F_C = Y$$

Subtracting,

$$\frac{1}{1-a} \qquad = (Y_1 - Y)$$

Since $1 > a > 0$, $1/(1 - a) > 1$, and $a/(1 - a) > 0$. Thus, if investment increases by one dollar, consumption increases, and national product thus increases by more than one dollar.

Problem Determine the effect of a one dollar increase in F_C upon Y and C.

In this Tiny Model, three features are presented that will characterize all the theories presented in this book:

(1) The model includes a definition of the part of the social accounts under discussion (here, $Y = C + I$), and a description of the behavior assumed to hold for the economic units in question (here, $C = aY + F_C$). This set of statements may be written in matrix-vector form, as a mapping of the variables [here the vector (Y, C)] into the factors [here the vector (I, F_C)].

(2) Corresponding to this mapping, an inverse mapping is derived, which carries the variables into the factors. In fact, the mapping associated with the theory is one-to-one. For every factor vector there is exactly one variable vector, and for every variable vector there is exactly one factor vector.

(3) All the statements in the theory are linear equations in the factors and variables.

By restricting our theories to linear theories, we are able to use simple mathematical methods of analyzing economic relations. We have reason to suppose that economic relations are nonlinear. (Fȯr example, in this theory, many economists feel that the larger Y is, the smaller a should be.) In this case, the analysis of the implications of the theory requires the use of the calculus. Theories that use the calculus have the interesting feature that when they are examined locally, they are linear. That is, if we choose some particular pair of initial values (Y_0, C_0) for the variables Y, C, and ask about the consequences of *small* changes in I and F_C, given that starting point, the analysis will be exactly like that of a linear theory.

VECTOR AND MATRIX NOTATION: TWO FORMS OF A THEORY

Each theory we shall discuss can be thought of in two ways, as was Tiny Model 1. A theory, in fact, involves some set of *factors* (such as I and F_C) which determine some set of *variables* (such as Y and C). The theory makes *behavioral sense* if it is written in one way, but to bring out its *economic usefulness*, it must be rewritten. The two ways of writing the theory are interchangeable, because one can be derived from the other.

The reasoning that has been applied to Tiny Model 1 can be applied to larger and more interesting theories, but it is convenient to present a compact way of writing a theory. We shall write the two forms of Tiny Model 1 as

$$(\mathbf{I}, \mathbf{F_C}) = (\mathbf{Y}, \mathbf{C}) \begin{pmatrix} 1 & -a \\ -1 & 1 \end{pmatrix} \tag{3.3}$$

and

$$(\mathbf{Y}, \mathbf{C}) = (\mathbf{I}, \mathbf{F_C}) \begin{pmatrix} \dfrac{1}{1-a} & \dfrac{a}{1-a} \\[2ex] \dfrac{1}{1-a} & \dfrac{1}{1-a} \end{pmatrix} \tag{3.4}$$

Any set of numbers, written (n_1, n_2, n_3, n_4, and so on) will be called a *vector*. In any theory, we associate a number in a given position with a particular element of the theory. Thus in (3.4), a vector $(\mathbf{Y}, \mathbf{C})$ consists of two numbers. If we saw the vector ($740,000,000,000, $620,000,000,000) in the context of (3.4) we would interpret this vector as the sentence "The national product is $740 billion and consumption is $620 billion."

Each theory in this book involves two vectors, a vector of *variables* and a vector of *factors*. The theory explains precisely how a vector of factors determines a vector of variables. In Tiny Model 1, the vector $(\mathbf{I}, \mathbf{F_C})$ determines the vector $(\mathbf{Y}, \mathbf{C})$ in the following sense: If I and F_C both have particular numerical values, then there is only one value that Y may have and one value that C may have.

The precise nature of the relation between the variables and the factors is specified by a pair of *matrices.* In (3.3), above, the matrix $\begin{pmatrix} 1 & -a \\ -1 & 1 \end{pmatrix}$ tells how to calculate the vector $(\mathbf{I}, \mathbf{F_C})$, which is the image of the vector $(\mathbf{Y}, \mathbf{C})$ under the mapping associated with the theory. The matrix

$$\begin{pmatrix} \dfrac{1}{1-a} & \dfrac{a}{1-a} \\ \dfrac{1}{1-a} & \dfrac{1}{1-a} \end{pmatrix}$$

tells how to calculate the vector $(\mathbf{Y}, \mathbf{C})$, which is the image of the vector $(\mathbf{I}, \mathbf{F_C})$ under the mapping associated with the theory. In describing Tiny Model 1, we started by writing down two pairs of linear equations. The matrices given in (3.3) and (3.4) are another, more compact way of describing the relationships involved.

The representation (3.3) is another way of writing the behavioral version (3.2) of Tiny Model 1 in the first part of this chapter. Two vectors, $(\mathbf{V_1}, \mathbf{V_2})$ and $(\mathbf{W_1}, \mathbf{W_2})$, are equal if $\mathbf{V_1} = \mathbf{W_1}$ and also $\mathbf{V_2} = \mathbf{W_2}$. The *image* of a vector under a matrix is given by

$$(\mathbf{V_1}, \mathbf{V_2}) \begin{pmatrix} a & b \\ c & d \end{pmatrix} = (\mathbf{aV_1} + \mathbf{cV_2}, \mathbf{bV_1} + \mathbf{dV_2})$$

Thus (3.3) states

$$(\mathbf{I}, \mathbf{F_C}) = (\mathbf{Y}, \mathbf{C}) \begin{pmatrix} 1 & -a \\ -1 & 1 \end{pmatrix} = (\mathbf{Y} - \mathbf{C}, -\mathbf{aY} + \mathbf{C})$$

When we compare the left vector and the right vector, we compare

$$I \text{ with } (Y - C)$$
$$F_C \text{ with } (-aY + C)$$

But in (3.2) we said these were two equalities.

On the other hand, (3.4) states

$$(\mathbf{Y}, \mathbf{C}) = (\mathbf{I}, \mathbf{F_C}) \begin{pmatrix} \dfrac{1}{1-a} & \dfrac{a}{1-a} \\ \dfrac{1}{1-a} & \dfrac{1}{1-a} \end{pmatrix}$$

$$= \left(\frac{1}{1-\mathbf{a}}\mathbf{I} + \frac{1}{1-\mathbf{a}}\mathbf{F_C}, \frac{\mathbf{a}}{1-\mathbf{a}}\mathbf{I} + \frac{1}{1-\mathbf{a}}\mathbf{F_C}\right)$$

When we compare the left vector with the right vector, we compare

$$Y \text{ with } \left(\frac{1}{1-a}I + \frac{1}{1-a}Fc\right)$$

$$C \text{ with } \left(\frac{a}{1-a}I + \frac{1}{1-a}Fc\right)$$

But in (3.1) we said that these were equalities.

Thus, any set of linear equations may be written in matrix-vector notation. For example,

$$u = Ax + By + Cz$$
$$v = Dx + Ey + Fz$$
$$w = Gx + Hy + Iz$$

may be written

$$(\mathbf{u}, \mathbf{v}, \mathbf{w}) = (\mathbf{x}, \mathbf{y}, \mathbf{z}) \begin{pmatrix} A & D & G \\ B & E & H \\ C & F & I \end{pmatrix} \tag{3.5}$$

The elements of column 1 of the matrix are the coefficients of the first equation; the elements of column 2 of the matrix are the coefficients of the second equation; the elements of column 3 are the coefficients of the third equation. And if this system of equations is a complete linear economic theory, involving a one-to-one relation between vectors of variables and vectors of factors, there would be an *inverse matrix* which would enable us to write

$$(\mathbf{x}, \mathbf{y}, \mathbf{z}) = (\mathbf{u}, \mathbf{v}, \mathbf{w}) \begin{pmatrix} A & D & G \\ B & E & H \\ C & F & I \end{pmatrix} \tag{3.6}$$

The matrix of Tiny Model 1 had two rows and two columns (and its inverse did, also). The matrix of (3.5) and its inverse in (3.6) have three rows and three columns. Matrices with n rows and n columns are called *square*; n is the *order* of the matrix.

However, not all matrices are square. The equation

$$(\mathbf{u}, \mathbf{v}) = (\mathbf{x}, \mathbf{y}, \mathbf{z}) \begin{pmatrix} A & D \\ B & E \\ C & F \end{pmatrix}$$

corresponds to the pair of equations

$$u = Ax + By + Cz$$
$$v = Dx + Ey + Fz$$

In this case, the matrix has three rows and two columns, and is called *rectangular*.

Rectangular matrices never have inverses; some square matrices do not have inverses. But a theory always has a matrix with an inverse. If it does not have an inverse, it is not possible to explain how changes in each factor affect each variable. To show that some set of equations is a theory, we simply write the matrix of the theory and show that it has an inverse.

There is a regular mathematical procedure for inverting matrices. It is rather tedious if the matrix is of order greater than 2. Consequently, when we present a theory, we shall ordinarily simply present inverse matrices without showing the calculations.

For a square matrix of order 2, the formula for the inverse is simple enough. The inverse of

$$M = \begin{pmatrix} a & b \\ c & d \end{pmatrix}$$

is

$$\begin{pmatrix} \dfrac{d}{ad-bc} & \dfrac{-b}{ad-bc} \\ \dfrac{-c}{ad-bc} & \dfrac{a}{ad-bc} \end{pmatrix}$$

providing $ad - bc \neq 0$. In the case of $ad - bc = 0$, the matrix has no inverse.

If $\mathbf{V} = (\mathbf{x}, \mathbf{y})$ is any vector with two components, its *image* under M is

$$VM = (\mathbf{x}, \mathbf{y}) \begin{pmatrix} a & b \\ c & d \end{pmatrix} = (\mathbf{ax} + \mathbf{cy}, \mathbf{bx} + \mathbf{dy}) = (\mathbf{x}', \mathbf{y}') = \mathbf{V}'$$

and the image of (x', y') under M^{-1} (the inverse of M) is

$$\mathbf{V}'\mathbf{M}^{-1} = (\mathbf{x}', \mathbf{y}') \begin{pmatrix} \dfrac{d}{ad-bc} & \dfrac{-b}{ad-bc} \\ \dfrac{-c}{ad-bc} & \dfrac{a}{ad-bc} \end{pmatrix} = \left(\frac{\mathbf{dx}' - \mathbf{cy}'}{\mathbf{ad} - \mathbf{bc}}, \frac{-\mathbf{bx}' + \mathbf{ay}'}{\mathbf{ad} - \mathbf{bc}} \right)$$

Now

$$\frac{dx' - cy'}{ad - bc} = \frac{d(ax + cy) - c(bx + dy)}{ad - bc} = \frac{(ad - bc)x + (cd - cd)y}{ad - bc} = x$$

$$\frac{-bx' + ay'}{ad - bc} = \frac{-b(ax + cy) + a(bx + dy)}{ad - bc} = \frac{(-ab + ab)x + (ad - bc)y}{ad - bc} = y$$

This result, $\mathbf{F} = \mathbf{VM} = (\mathbf{FM}^{-1})\mathbf{M} = \mathbf{F}(\mathbf{M}^{-1}\mathbf{M}) = \mathbf{F}$, has been shown for matrices of order 2, operating on vectors with two components. For larger theories, having an arbitrary number of variables and matrices of the same orders, an exactly similar result holds, although it is more work to demonstrate it in the manner shown here.

Remark about Notation

Some readers may have been taught a slightly different way of writing vectors and matrices. Although *row* vectors, like $(\mathbf{V}_1, \mathbf{V}_2, \mathbf{V}_3)$, are used here, some readers may be accustomed to *column* vectors:

$$\begin{pmatrix} \mathbf{V}_1 \\ \mathbf{V}_2 \\ \mathbf{V}_3 \end{pmatrix}$$

Also, although this book writes

$$(\mathbf{V}_1, \mathbf{V}_2, \mathbf{V}_3) \begin{pmatrix} A & B & C \\ D & E & F \\ G & H & J \end{pmatrix}$$
$$= (\mathbf{AV}_1 + \mathbf{DV}_2 + \mathbf{GV}_3, \mathbf{BV}_1 + \mathbf{EV}_2 + \mathbf{HV}_3, \mathbf{CV}_1 + \mathbf{FV}_2 + \mathbf{JV}_3)$$

they will be accustomed to writing

$$\begin{pmatrix} A & D & G \\ B & E & H \\ C & F & J \end{pmatrix} \begin{pmatrix} \mathbf{V}_1 \\ \mathbf{V}_2 \\ \mathbf{V}_3 \end{pmatrix} = \begin{pmatrix} \mathbf{AV}_1 + \mathbf{DV}_2 + \mathbf{GV}_3 \\ \mathbf{BV}_1 + \mathbf{EV}_2 + \mathbf{HV}_3 \\ \mathbf{CV}_1 + \mathbf{FV}_2 + \mathbf{JV}_3 \end{pmatrix}$$

As such readers can see, the difference in notation is the following: (1) Vectors are rows in this book, not columns; (2) matrices appear on the right side of vectors in this book, not the left; and (3) a given matrix in this book is the "transpose" of the matrix the reader might expect. In the example above, our matrix has *row 1* with elements *A, B, C*. The reader would expect these elements in *column 1*.

If we had written the matrices in the manner that these readers were familiar with, we would have displeased other readers. It also seems to be easier to set type in this notation.

TWO MORE TINY MODELS

Tiny Model 2

Tiny Model 2 does for the balance sheet accounts what Tiny Model 1 did for national income. It is the simplest theory about its subject known to man. We start off by asserting that there are two kinds of assets: cash, and plant and equipment, and that there is no debt. Thus the balance sheet is

Cash,	M	Net worth,	W
Plant and equipment,	K		

This balance sheet indicates

$$W = M + K$$

Now suppose that the community's demand for plant and equipment depends partly on total assets, so that

$$K = bW + F_K$$

This second statement is about plant and equipment: Two things affect the amount of plant that people wish to own. One of these is their total wealth, the other is "business tastes." The two are "additive": bW is the holding of plant which is induced by wealth. We suspect that the coefficient b is between 0 and 1. It is positive because we suspect that if people have a larger amount of assets, they will want more plant. It is less than 1 because we suspect that if people have a larger amount of assets, they will also want more cash. The demand for money, of course, is

$$\begin{aligned} M &= W - K \\ &= W - bW - F_K \\ &= (1 - b)W - F_K \end{aligned}$$

Therefore, if businesses hold more plant as their assets grow, $b > 0$; if they also hold more cash as their assets grow, $(1 - b) > 0$, so that $1 > b > 0$.

F_K is an indicator of the amount of "autonomous" plant holdings. We shall think of changes in business habits as taking place in F_K rather than in b.

Now let us express Tiny Model 2 in vector-matrix form. There are two factors, M and F_K; two variables, K and W; and the two forms of the theory are

$$(\mathbf{M}, \mathbf{F_K}) = (\mathbf{W}, \mathbf{K}) \begin{pmatrix} 1 & -b \\ -1 & 1 \end{pmatrix}$$

$$(\mathbf{W}, \mathbf{K}) = (\mathbf{M}, \mathbf{F_K}) \begin{pmatrix} \dfrac{1}{1-b} & \dfrac{b}{1-b} \\ \dfrac{1}{1-b} & \dfrac{1}{1-b} \end{pmatrix}$$

The reader with a good memory will have noticed that this section of the chapter is almost verbatim the same as the first section, except that

M has replaced I
F_K has replaced F_C
W has replaced Y
K has replaced C
b has replaced a

In other words, these theories have similar structure, although they are about different sectors of the economy. The similarity of structure is emphasized by the similarity of the two matrices; the difference in subject is shown by comparing the names of the variables and factors.

Clearly it is a great advantage to have a uniform way of looking at different parts of the economy, if it makes sense. We shall naturally try to use a uniform approach, although we shall not always be able to stick to it.

Problem Suppose that more money is created simply by having more printed on printing presses. Show the effect on total assets and on plant of printing one paper dollar.

Problem Suppose that "autonomous plant" (F_K) increases by \$1.00. What is the effect on total assets and on plant?

Tiny Model 3

A large part of microeconomics is concerned with the "theory of price formation." Although microeconomics does not, strictly speaking, concern us it is useful to present Tiny Model 3, which is a theory of what the price and quantity traded will be in the case of a single, arbitrarily selected commodity. The case selected for examination is that of the "isolated market"—what goes on in such a market is completely independent of what goes on in other markets.

For present purposes, the basic hypotheses are:

(1) The amount that buyers are willing to buy depends on the price they must pay: the higher the price, the *less* buyers will want. Specifically:

$$q_D = ep_D + F_D \qquad (e < 0)$$

The subscript D stands for demand. The factor F_D is called the *level of demand* and stands for everything (income, taste, fashion, whim) other than price which affects consumer willingness to buy.

(2) The amount that sellers are willing to sell depends on the price that they receive when they sell: The higher the price, the *more* sellers will want to sell. Specifically:

$$q_s = fp_s + F_S \qquad (f > 0)$$

The subscript s stands for supply. The factor F_S is called the *level of supply* and stands for everything other than price which affects the willingness of sellers to sell.

(3) The price buyers pay is equal to the price sellers receive. That is, we ignore taxes, dealers' commissions, delivery costs, and so on. That is, $p_D = p_s = p$.

(4) The market is functioning satisfactorily only if everyone who wants to

buy can find a willing seller, and everyone who wants to sell can find a willing buyer. If this condition is met,[2] then $q_D = q_s = q$.

Given these four conditions,

$$F_D = q - ep$$

$$F_S = q - fp$$

This means that p, the *equilibrium price*, and q, the *equilibrium quantity*, are given by inverting the relation:

$$(\mathbf{F_D}, \mathbf{F_S}) = (q, p)\begin{pmatrix} 1 & 1 \\ -e & -f \end{pmatrix}$$

that is, by

$$(\mathbf{F_D}, \mathbf{F_S})\begin{pmatrix} \dfrac{-f}{e-f} & \dfrac{-1}{e-f} \\ \dfrac{e}{e-f} & \dfrac{1}{e-f} \end{pmatrix} = (\mathbf{q}, \mathbf{p})$$

That is, there is a single price and a single quantity that can exist in a market in which conditions (1) to (4) hold, and in which the levels of demand and supply (F_D and F_S) are given.

Problem What are the effects on quantity and on price of an increase of 1 in F_D? Are these increases or decreases?

Problem What are the effects on quantity and on price of an increase of 1 in F_S? Are these increases or decreases?

USEFUL PROPOSITIONS ABOUT VECTORS AND MATRICES

Addition and Subtraction of Vectors

Suppose that Tiny Model 3 is true and we look at this particular market at two different dates. The demand equation will be

$$F_{D1} = q_1 - ep_1$$

at time 1, and

$$F_{D2} = q_2 - ep_2$$

[2] Observe that the converse is not necessarily true. Even if $q_D = q_s$, it may be that communications in the market are such that some buyers do not have access to all sellers, or some sellers do not have access to all buyers. In this case, the market may not work satisfactorily because willing buyers and sellers cannot find each other.

The difference between these two observations is

$$\Delta F_D = \Delta q - e\Delta p$$

where Δ means "the change in," so that

$$\Delta F_D = F_{D2} - F_{D1}$$

$$\Delta q = q_2 - q_1$$

$$\Delta p = p_2 - p_1$$

Similarly, the supply equation at the two dates will be

$$F_{S1} = q_1 - fp_1$$

$$F_{S2} = q_2 - fp_2$$

so that

$$\Delta F_S = \Delta q - f\Delta p$$

If these two expressions are written in vector matrix form,

$$(\Delta \mathbf{F_D}, \Delta \mathbf{F_S}) = (\Delta \mathbf{q}, \Delta \mathbf{p}) \begin{pmatrix} 1 & 1 \\ -e & -f \end{pmatrix}$$

Notice that the structure of this equation is exactly the same as the structure of the original form of the theory. That is, the matrix is exactly the same as before. Likewise, the inverse equation relating *changes* in factors to *changes* in variables,

$$(\Delta \mathbf{q}, \Delta \mathbf{p}) = (\Delta \mathbf{F_D}, \Delta \mathbf{F_S}) \begin{pmatrix} \frac{-f}{e-f} & \frac{-1}{e-f} \\ \frac{e}{e-f} & \frac{1}{e-f} \end{pmatrix}$$

is of exactly the same structure as the corresponding relation between factors and variables.

This result is true of vectors of any order. If $\mathbf{F}_1 = (\mathbf{f}_1, \mathbf{f}_2, \cdots, \mathbf{f}_n)$ and $\mathbf{F}_2 = (\mathbf{f}_1', \mathbf{f}_2', \cdots, \mathbf{f}_n')$ are vectors of the same order, then $\Delta\mathbf{F}$ is defined as the vector $(\mathbf{f}_1' - \mathbf{f}_1, \mathbf{f}_2' - \mathbf{f}_2, \cdots, \mathbf{f}_n' - \mathbf{f}_n) = (\Delta\mathbf{f}_1, \Delta\mathbf{f}_2, \cdots, \Delta\mathbf{f}_n)$. If $\mathbf{M}$ is a matrix, such that $\mathbf{F} = \mathbf{VM}$, then $\mathbf{F}_1 = \mathbf{V}_1\mathbf{M}$ and $\mathbf{F}_2 = \mathbf{V}_2\mathbf{M}$ mean that $\Delta\mathbf{F} = \Delta\mathbf{VM}$; moreover $\Delta\mathbf{V} = \Delta\mathbf{FM}^{-1}$, where $\mathbf{M}^{-1}$ is the inverse of $\mathbf{M}$.

The theories used in this book are all *linear*. Theories that are linear (and only such theories) have the notable feature that a single structure is common to the relation between factors and variables, and the relation between *changes* in factors and *changes* in variables. Thus linear theories are particularly easy to use, and particularly suitable for beginners.

Our operations on vectors and matrices of every order are simply applications of the following three rules:

(1) If a is a number and $\mathbf{V} = (\mathbf{V}_1 \cdots \mathbf{V}_n)$ a vector, then $\mathbf{aV}$ is the vector $(\mathbf{aV}_1, \mathbf{aV}_2, \cdots, \mathbf{aV}_n)$.

(2) If $\mathbf{V} = (\mathbf{V}_1, \mathbf{V}_2, \cdots, \mathbf{V}_n)$ and $\mathbf{W} = (\mathbf{W}_1, \mathbf{W}_2, \cdots, \mathbf{W}_n)$ are vectors of the same order, then $\mathbf{V} + \mathbf{W}$ is the vector

$$(\mathbf{V}_1 + \mathbf{W}_1, \mathbf{V}_2 + \mathbf{W}_2, \cdots, \mathbf{V}_n + \mathbf{W}_n).$$

(3) If $\mathbf{V}$, $\mathbf{W}$ are vectors and M is a matrix, then

$$\mathbf{VM} + \mathbf{WM} = (\mathbf{V} + \mathbf{W})\mathbf{M}$$

The Economic Interpretation of the Inverse Matrix

Theories consist of pairs of matrix equations:

$$\mathbf{F} = \mathbf{VM}$$
$$\mathbf{V} = \mathbf{FM}^{-1}$$

Here $\mathbf{F}$ is a vector of factors which are taken to be given, and which collectively determine $\mathbf{V}$, a vector of economic variables. From such a pair, as we have just seen, we can derive the pair

$$\Delta\mathbf{F} = \Delta\mathbf{VM}$$
$$\Delta\mathbf{V} = \Delta\mathbf{FM}^{-1}$$

Any vector

$$\Delta\mathbf{F} = (\Delta\mathbf{f}_1, \Delta\mathbf{f}_2, \cdots, \Delta\mathbf{f}_n)$$

may be thought of as the sum of the vectors

$$\begin{aligned}
\Delta\mathbf{F}_1 &= (\Delta\mathbf{f}_1, \mathbf{0}, \mathbf{0}, \cdots, \mathbf{0}) \\
\Delta\mathbf{F}_2 &= (\mathbf{0}, \Delta\mathbf{f}_2, \mathbf{0}, \cdots, \mathbf{0}) \\
\Delta\mathbf{F}_3 &= (\mathbf{0}, \mathbf{0}, \Delta\mathbf{f}_3, \cdots, \mathbf{0}) \\
&\cdots \\
\Delta\mathbf{F}_n &= (\mathbf{0}, \mathbf{0}, \mathbf{0}, \cdots, \Delta\mathbf{f}_n)
\end{aligned}$$

Each of these vectors is associated with the following economic event: *one* factor, and only one factor changes. Consequently, if

$$\Delta\mathbf{V} = \Delta\mathbf{FM}^{-1}$$

we may write this as the sum of the effects of the isolated changes:

$$\begin{aligned}
\Delta\mathbf{V} &= \Delta\mathbf{V}_1 + \Delta\mathbf{V}_2 + \cdots + \Delta\mathbf{V}_n = \Delta\mathbf{F}_1\mathbf{M}^{-1} + \Delta\mathbf{F}_2\mathbf{M}^{-1} + \cdots + \Delta\mathbf{F}_n\mathbf{M}^{-1} \\
&= (\Delta\mathbf{F}_1 + \Delta\mathbf{F}_2 + \cdots + \Delta\mathbf{F}_n)\mathbf{M}^{-1} = \Delta\mathbf{FM}^{-1}
\end{aligned}$$

This is true because

$$\begin{aligned}
\Delta\mathbf{V}_1 &= \Delta\mathbf{F}_1\mathbf{M}^{-1} \\
\Delta\mathbf{V}_2 &= \Delta\mathbf{F}_2\mathbf{M}^{-1} \\
&\cdots \\
\Delta\mathbf{V}_n &= \Delta\mathbf{F}_n\mathbf{M}^{-1}
\end{aligned}$$

When we calculate $\Delta\mathbf{F}_i\mathbf{M}^{-1}$ (i is any one of the numbers $1 \cdots n$), so as to obtain $\Delta\mathbf{V}_i$, we are calculating the effects which a change in $\mathbf{F}_i$ has upon each of the variables in the theory.

We write out $\Delta \mathbf{F}_i \mathbf{M}^{-1} = \Delta \mathbf{V}_i$ in full:

$$(\mathbf{0}, \cdots, \mathbf{0}, \Delta \mathbf{f}_i, \mathbf{0}, \cdots, \mathbf{0}) \begin{pmatrix} m_{11} & m_{12} & \cdots & m_{1n} \\ m_{21} & m_{22} & \cdots & m_{2n} \\ & \cdots & & \\ m_{i1} & m_{i2} & \cdots & m_{in} \\ & \cdots & & \\ m_{n1} & m_{n2} & \cdots & m_{nn} \end{pmatrix}$$

$$= (\mathbf{m}_{i1}\Delta \mathbf{f}_i, \mathbf{m}_{i2}\Delta \mathbf{f}_i, \cdots, \mathbf{m}_{in}\Delta \mathbf{f}_i)$$
$$= (\Delta \mathbf{V}_1{}^{(i)}, \Delta \mathbf{V}_2{}^{(i)}, \cdots, \Delta \mathbf{V}_n{}^{(i)})$$

(Here m_{ij} is the element in row i, column j of M^{-1}.) Therefore,

$$\begin{aligned} \Delta V_1{}^{(i)} &= m_{i1}\Delta f_i \\ \Delta V_2{}^{(i)} &= m_{i2}\Delta f_i \\ &\cdots \\ \Delta V_n{}^{(i)} &= m_{in}\Delta f_i \end{aligned}$$

If f_i changes by one unit, we have $\Delta f_i = 1$; then these equations become

$$\begin{aligned} \Delta V_1{}^{(i)} &= m_{i1} = \text{the effect on } V_1 \text{ of a unit change in } f_i \\ \Delta V_2{}^{(i)} &= m_{i2} = \text{the effect on } V_2 \text{ of a unit change in } f_i \\ &\cdots \\ \Delta V_n{}^{(i)} &= m_{in} = \text{the effect on } V_n \text{ of a unit change in } f_i \end{aligned}$$

The problems presented in the discussion of Tiny Models 1–3 involved special cases of this proposition.

We are interested in the inverse matrix of a theory because the elements of this inverse matrix measure the effects of unit changes in the factors upon the variables of the theory. This interpretation makes the matrix into a set of propositions implied by the theorem.

In the future, when a theory has been written both ways (that is, both as a variable-into-factor mapping and as an "inverse," or factor-into-variable mapping), a table of *implications* will be given. For Tiny Model 3, for instance, the table would appear as shown in Table 3.1.

Table 3.1. The Implications of Tiny Model 3

THE EFFECT OF A UNIT CHANGE IN	*The Effect of a Unit Change upon*	
	QUANTITY (q)	PRICE (p)
The level of demand (ΔF_D)	$\frac{-f}{e-f}$	$\frac{-1}{e-f}$
The level of supply (ΔF_S)	$\frac{e}{e-f}$	$\frac{1}{e-f}$

Block Notation and the Inversion of Larger Matrices

Matrices have been considered as arrays of numbers. Suppose, however, that we can construct two theories, both mapping vectors of factors into vectors of variables in one-to-one fashion. Then for each theory there will be an invertible matrix, say,

$$M_1 = \begin{pmatrix} a_{11} & a_{12} & \cdots & a_{1n} \\ a_{21} & a_{22} & \cdots & a_{2n} \\ & \cdots & & \\ a_{n1} & a_{n2} & \cdots & a_{nn} \end{pmatrix} \qquad M_2 = \begin{pmatrix} b_{11} & b_{12} & \cdots & b_{1n} \\ b_{21} & b_{22} & \cdots & b_{2n} \\ & & \cdots & \\ b_{n1} & b_{n2} & \cdots & b_{nn} \end{pmatrix}$$

It may be that these theories have some parts in common. These parts might consist of certain statements common to both. This similarity would be reflected by the fact that certain columns of M_1 would have the same elements as the corresponding columns of M_2. Alternatively certain *blocks* of elements reappear in several theories, including theories involving matrices of different orders.

For example, in Chapter 6, we consider matrices of the form:

$$\begin{pmatrix} M_{11} & M_{12} \\ M_{21} & M_{22} \end{pmatrix}$$

in which the symbol M_{ij} stands for a square or rectangular block of numbers. For instance, M_{11} may be the matrix

$$\begin{pmatrix} 1 & -a \\ -1 & 1 \end{pmatrix}$$

of Tiny Model 1, and M_{22} may be the matrix

$$\begin{pmatrix} 1 & -b \\ -1 & 1 \end{pmatrix}$$

of Tiny Model 2. Written as a mapping, the theory takes the form

$$(\mathbf{F}_1, \mathbf{F}_2) \begin{pmatrix} M_{11} & M_{12} \\ M_{21} & M_{22} \end{pmatrix} = (\mathbf{V}_1, \mathbf{V}_2) \tag{3.7}$$

However, $\mathbf{F}_1$, $\mathbf{F}_2$, $\mathbf{V}_1$, $\mathbf{V}_2$ do not stand for single numbers, but rather for sets of numbers. A special case of (3.7) is the theory

$$(\mathbf{F}_1, \mathbf{F}_2) \begin{pmatrix} M_{11} & 0 \\ 0 & M_{22} \end{pmatrix} = (\mathbf{V}_1, \mathbf{V}_2) \tag{3.8}$$

(Here the symbols "0" stand for blocks of zeros.) Theory (3.8) may be written out in the form

$$\begin{aligned} \mathbf{F}_1\mathbf{M}_{11} &= \mathbf{V}_1 \\ \mathbf{F}_2\mathbf{M}_{22} &= \mathbf{V}_2 \end{aligned} \tag{3.9}$$

This statement says that $\mathbf{V}_1$ depends only on the factors listed in $\mathbf{F}_1$; $\mathbf{V}_2$ depends only on the factors listed in $\mathbf{F}_2$. In contrast, the theory (3.7) states

$$\mathbf{F}_1\mathbf{M}_{11} + \mathbf{F}_2\mathbf{M}_{21} = \mathbf{V}_1$$
$$\mathbf{F}_1\mathbf{M}_{12} + \mathbf{F}_2\mathbf{M}_{22} = \mathbf{V}_2$$

That is, the factors listed in $\mathbf{F}_2$ affect $\mathbf{V}_1$ and the factors listed in $\mathbf{F}_1$ affect $\mathbf{V}_2$. Even so, the more complicated first theory, (3.7), may have certain blocks in common with the simpler theory, (3.8).

The nondiagonal blocks M_{12} and M_{21} basically consist of linkages between "little" theories pertaining only to part of the variables and part of the factors in the system.

A matrix written in *block form* always has square diagonal blocks. (These are the blocks M_{11}, M_{22}.) Nondiagonal blocks (the blocks M_{12} and M_{21}) may be rectangular. For example, a block matrix may have the following structure:

$$\begin{array}{cccc} & \text{2 columns} & \text{3 columns} & \\ M = & \Big(M_{11} & M_{12} \Big) & \text{2 rows} \\ & \Big(M_{21} & M_{22} \Big) & \text{3 rows} \end{array}$$

In this case, the blocks making up the vectors must be defined so that multiplication is possible: in $\mathbf{F} = (\mathbf{F}_1, \mathbf{F}_2)$, $\mathbf{F}_1$ must have two components and $\mathbf{F}_2$ must have 3 components if the vector $\mathbf{FM}$ is to be calculated according to the rules set forth above.

There are two reasons for using block notation in matrices. The first is economic: Where successive theories contain elements in common, the matrices associated with the theories have blocks in common. This notation emphasizes the similarity. The second reason is computational: It is much easier to calculate the inverse of a large matrix if smaller parts of it have already been inverted. It is convenient to start with a small block, and to invert the matrix in steps.

The block matrix

$$\begin{pmatrix} M_{11} & 0 \\ 0 & M_{22} \end{pmatrix}$$

is called *block-diagonal*. The block matrices

$$\begin{pmatrix} M_{11} & M_{12} \\ 0 & M_{22} \end{pmatrix} \quad \text{and} \quad \begin{pmatrix} M_{11} & 0 \\ M_{21} & M_{22} \end{pmatrix}$$

are called *block-triangular*. If a matrix is block-diagonal or block-triangular, its inverse may be broken into zero and nonzero blocks in exactly the same way.[3]

It is much easier to invert block-diagonal and block-triangular matrices than other matrices. For this reason, simple theories are apt to involve such

[3] However, if some individual element of a nonzero block happens to be zero, the corresponding element of the inverse will not necessarily be zero.

matrices. We shall consider why theories of this sort may be less useful as descriptions of the economy than as learning aids.

Sometimes a theory is written in a form that does not seem to be block-triangular, but can be made block-triangular. Thus the matrix

$$(\mathbf{F}_1, \mathbf{F}_2, \mathbf{F}_3, \mathbf{F}_4) \begin{pmatrix} I & 0 & 0 & J \\ G & F & E & H \\ C & B & A & D \\ K & 0 & 0 & L \end{pmatrix} = (\mathbf{V}_1, \mathbf{V}_2, \mathbf{V}_3, \mathbf{V}_4) \tag{3.10}$$

looks as if it were *not* block-triangular. However, if the variables are rearranged so that the vector variable becomes $(\mathbf{V}_2, \mathbf{V}_3, \mathbf{V}_1, \mathbf{V}_4)$, the columns of the matrix must also be rearranged:

$$(\mathbf{F}_1, \mathbf{F}_2, \mathbf{F}_3, \mathbf{F}_4) \begin{pmatrix} 0 & 0 & I & J \\ F & E & G & H \\ B & A & C & D \\ 0 & 0 & K & L \end{pmatrix} = (\mathbf{V}_2, \mathbf{V}_3, \mathbf{V}_1, \mathbf{V}_4)$$

Now rearrange the order of the factors, so that the factor vector becomes $(\mathbf{F}_2, \mathbf{F}_3, \mathbf{F}_1, \mathbf{F}_4)$. Then the rows of the matrix must also be rearranged:

$$(\mathbf{F}_2, \mathbf{F}_3, \mathbf{F}_1, \mathbf{F}_4) \begin{pmatrix} F & E & G & H \\ B & A & C & D \\ 0 & 0 & I & J \\ 0 & 0 & K & L \end{pmatrix} = (\mathbf{V}_2, \mathbf{V}_3, \mathbf{V}_1, \mathbf{V}_4) \tag{3.11}$$

The matrix is now in block-triangular form. It is much easier to invert (3.11) than to invert (3.10), although the two say the same thing.

Problem Verify the statement that (3.10) and (3.11) are the same theory.

Our work proceeds by a process of gradual escalation. Consequently, theories involving matrices such as

$$\begin{pmatrix} M_{11} & M_{12} & M_{13} \\ M_{21} & M_{22} & M_{23} \\ M_{31} & M_{32} & M_{33} \end{pmatrix}$$

will usually turn out to be expressible as

$$\begin{pmatrix} \bar{M}_{11} & \bar{M}_{12} \\ \bar{M}_{21} & \bar{M}_{22} \end{pmatrix} \quad \text{where} \quad \bar{M}_{11} = \begin{pmatrix} M_{11} & M_{12} \\ M_{21} & M_{22} \end{pmatrix}$$

$$\bar{M}_{12} = \begin{pmatrix} M_{13} \\ M_{23} \end{pmatrix}$$

$$\bar{M}_{21} = (M_{31} \quad M_{32})$$

$$\bar{M}_{22} = (M_{33})$$

some parts of which have already been studied.

The general mathematical formulas for inverting matrices become very complicated indeed. The matrices presented here are usually rather simple to invert, because:

(1) In a general mathematical formula for inverting large matrices, each element of a matrix is treated as an arbitrary number. A theory usually specifies that many elements of the matrix are zero or one, and thus simplifies the task of inversion.
(2) The whole purpose of a theory is to present a simple way of looking at a complicated problem. The simpler a theory is, the smaller the number of connections asserted to exist between pairs of variables; and hence, the larger the number of zero elements in the matrix expressing the theory.
(3) A book of *simple* economic theory will present theories involving a relatively small number of variables; and each theory will involve a relatively small number of connections among the variables. That is, simple theories mean large numbers of ones and zeros in the matrix expressing the theory. The larger the number of ones and zeros, the easier it is to invert a matrix.
(4) Even simple theories can be useful in understanding the economy, if they make good use of the basic concepts of social accounting, and if they express in some elementary form the principal ideas that economists have developed over the years.

How to Test an Inverse Matrix Given in This Book

Readers of this book do not have to invert matrices themselves. But they may wonder whether they should believe an author who says, "The inverse of that horrible matrix is *this*" and then simply points to a matrix with no further explanation. Inverting a matrix is not a magical art, and verifying the claim that one matrix is the inverse of another is straightforward.

Remember, of course, that not all matrices have inverses. If they do not, however, there is something the matter with an economic theory associated with it. Anyone who sets up his own theory, therefore, must verify that it has an inverse. Otherwise, he can show that there is more than one solution to his problem.

First, it is easy to see that there is a matrix that is like the number 1 in the following sense: If n is *any* number, $n \times 1 = n$. There is a matrix E_m of every order m, which is like 1 in the sense that $\mathbf{V}E_m = \mathbf{V}$ for every vector with m components. Let $m = 4$. Then

$$E_4 = \begin{pmatrix} 1 & 0 & 0 & 0 \\ 0 & 1 & 0 & 0 \\ 0 & 0 & 1 & 0 \\ 0 & 0 & 0 & 1 \end{pmatrix}$$

Problem Verify that $\mathbf{VE}_4 = \mathbf{V}$, whatever the four components of **V** may be.

The matrix E_m is called *the unit matrix of order m*. Usually "of order *m*" may be dropped in this book, for it will be clear from the context what the order of the matrix is.

Second, suppose we start with a theory which says $\mathbf{F} = \mathbf{VM}$, where **F** and **V** are vectors and **M** is a matrix. Then the inverse of **M**, which is written $\mathbf{M}^{-1}$, is such that

$$\mathbf{V} = \mathbf{FM}^{-1}$$

But we may substitute for **F**, obtaining

$$\mathbf{V} = \mathbf{VMM}^{-1}$$

What is the meaning of MM^{-1}, two matrices written side-by-side in this way? If V and M were numbers, then M^{-1} would be the reciprocal of M, namely $1/M$, and (MM^{-1}) would be a product, $M \times (1/M) = 1$. Analogously, for matrices, MM^{-1} stands for multiplication of matrices. What we need, then, is a way of multiplying matrices. Given such a way, the reader may check for himself to see whether the author is right in claiming that some matrix is the inverse of some other matrix.

Third, matrices are multiplied together by the following rule: *The product of two matrices is itself a matrix.* For example, suppose we multiply the following pair of matrices, and obtain the product $AB = C$, written as

$$\begin{pmatrix} a_{11} & a_{12} & a_{13} \\ a_{21} & a_{22} & a_{23} \\ a_{31} & a_{32} & a_{33} \end{pmatrix} \begin{pmatrix} b_{11} & b_{12} & b_{13} \\ b_{21} & b_{22} & b_{23} \\ b_{31} & b_{32} & b_{33} \end{pmatrix} = \begin{pmatrix} c_{11} & c_{12} & c_{13} \\ c_{21} & c_{22} & c_{23} \\ c_{31} & c_{32} & c_{33} \end{pmatrix}$$

Here there are *two* subscripts to each element in each matrix. These subscripts are an address, telling where in the matrix the element is located. That is, a_{11} is in row 1, column 1; b_{23} is in row 2, column 3; and c_{31} is in row 3, column 1. (In this example the first subscript is the *row* address, the second is the *column* address.)

Take any element c_{ij}. i and j may be any pair of numbers from the set 1, 2, 3. Then matrix multiplication is defined by the rule

$$c_{ij} = a_{i1}b_{1j} + a_{i2}b_{2j} + a_{i3}b_{3j}$$

That is, take each element of the ith row of A, multiply it by the corresponding element of the jth column of B, and add the products.

If A and B were matrices of order 5, the same rule would be followed, but the list of terms would be longer:

$$c_{ij} = a_{i1}b_{1j} + a_{i2}b_{2j} + a_{i3}b_{3j} + a_{i4}b_{4j} + a_{i5}b_{5j}$$

and so on, for matrices of every order.

Fourth, in particular, if M is multiplied by its inverse, the product will be a unit matrix. Here are some easy examples of inverses, which readers should check for themselves:

$$\begin{pmatrix} a & 0 & 0 & 0 \\ 0 & b & 0 & 0 \\ 0 & 0 & c & 0 \\ 0 & 0 & 0 & d \end{pmatrix} \begin{pmatrix} 1/a & 0 & 0 & 0 \\ 0 & 1/b & 0 & 0 \\ 0 & 0 & 1/c & 0 \\ 0 & 0 & 0 & 1/d \end{pmatrix} = \begin{pmatrix} 1 & 0 & 0 & 0 \\ 0 & 1 & 0 & 0 \\ 0 & 0 & 1 & 0 \\ 0 & 0 & 0 & 1 \end{pmatrix}$$

$$\begin{pmatrix} 1 & a & b \\ 0 & 1 & 0 \\ 0 & 0 & 1 \end{pmatrix} \begin{pmatrix} 1 & -a & -b \\ 0 & 1 & 0 \\ 0 & 0 & 1 \end{pmatrix} = \begin{pmatrix} 1 & 0 & 0 \\ 0 & 1 & 0 \\ 0 & 0 & 1 \end{pmatrix}$$

$$\begin{pmatrix} 1 & -a \\ -1 & 1 \end{pmatrix} \begin{pmatrix} \dfrac{1}{1-a} & \dfrac{a}{1-a} \\ \dfrac{1}{1-a} & \dfrac{1}{1-a} \end{pmatrix} = \begin{pmatrix} 1 & 0 \\ 0 & 1 \end{pmatrix}$$

(Notice that if $a = 1$, the second left matrix is not defined, because numbers may not be divided by zero. Therefore, if $a = 1$, the first left matrix has no inverse.)

$$\begin{pmatrix} a & b \\ c & d \end{pmatrix} \begin{pmatrix} \dfrac{d}{ad-bc} & \dfrac{-b}{ad-bc} \\ \dfrac{-c}{ad-bc} & \dfrac{a}{ad-bc} \end{pmatrix} = \begin{pmatrix} 1 & 0 \\ 0 & 1 \end{pmatrix}$$

(This gives the general formula for inverses of matrices of order 2, except when $ad = bc$. If the equality holds, the first left matrix has no inverse.)

$$\begin{pmatrix} 1 & -a & 0 & 0 \\ -1 & 1 & 0 & 0 \\ -1 & 0 & 1 & 0 \\ 0 & -b & -d & 1 \end{pmatrix} \begin{pmatrix} \dfrac{1}{1-a} & \dfrac{a}{1-a} & 0 & 0 \\ \dfrac{1}{1-a} & \dfrac{1}{1-a} & 0 & 0 \\ \dfrac{1}{1-a} & \dfrac{a}{1-a} & 1 & 0 \\ \dfrac{b+d}{1-a} & \dfrac{b+ad}{1-a} & d & 1 \end{pmatrix} = \begin{pmatrix} 1 & 0 & 0 & 0 \\ 0 & 1 & 0 & 0 \\ 0 & 0 & 1 & 0 \\ 0 & 0 & 0 & 1 \end{pmatrix}$$

Footnote for students of calculus. If consumption were a *nonlinear* function of income, Tiny Model 1 would become

$$Y = C + I$$
$$C = f(Y, \theta)$$

Here θ is a parameter of f. Then if I and θ are given,

$$Y = f(Y, \theta) + I$$

or

$$0 = g(Y, \theta, I)$$

If this is true, Y is implicitly a function of θ and I. In the neighborhood of a solution of this system,

$$dY = dC + dI$$

$$dC = \frac{\partial C}{\partial Y} dY + \frac{\partial C}{\partial \theta} d\theta$$

Here $\partial C/\partial \theta$ may be set equal to 1 by suitably scaling θ. Rearranging these terms

$$dI = dY + dC$$

$$d\theta = -\frac{\partial C}{\partial Y} dY + dC$$

In matrix-vector notation

$$(\mathbf{dI}, \mathbf{d\theta}) = (\mathbf{dY}, \mathbf{dC}) \begin{pmatrix} 1 & -1 \\ -\dfrac{\partial C}{\partial Y} & 1 \end{pmatrix}$$

In particular, when C is a linear function of Y, $\partial C/\partial Y$ is a constant, which is denoted by a in this book.

In other words, the coefficients that appear in a matrix may be thought of as the partial derivatives of functions. By limiting the discussion to linear functions, the theories in this book become particularly simple. Properties that otherwise would be true only in the neighborhood of a point hold true everywhere because the functions used have no bends in them.

In the nonlinear case, the inverse mapping

$$(\mathbf{dI}, \mathbf{d\theta}) \begin{pmatrix} \dfrac{1}{1 - \partial C/\partial Y} & \dfrac{\partial C/\partial Y}{1 - \partial C/\partial Y} \\ \dfrac{1}{1 - \partial C/\partial Y} & \dfrac{1}{1 - \partial C/\partial Y} \end{pmatrix} = (\mathbf{dY}, \mathbf{dC})$$

would be used to express Y and C explicitly as functions of I and θ:

$$Y = \int dY = \int \left(\frac{1}{1 - \partial C/\partial Y}\right) dI + \int \left(\frac{1}{1 - \partial C/\partial Y}\right) d\theta$$

$$C = \int dC = \int \left(\frac{\partial C/\partial Y}{1 - \partial C/\partial Y}\right) dI + \int \left(\frac{1}{1 - \partial C/\partial Y}\right) d\theta$$

But it is not necessary to go into these more difficult mathematical problems where linear functions are involved.

4

THE LEVEL OF THE NATIONAL PRODUCT

THE ORGANIZATION OF THE REST OF THE BOOK

Two subjects have been discussed: What is a social accounting system? And what is a theory? The social accounts were shown to consist of two interrelated sets of records: the national income and the national balance sheet. In discussing theories, three simple Tiny Models were presented; one dealt with the national product, the other with the national balance sheet.

The national income and national balance sheet will form the major unifying theme of this book. Their relative roles in determining what people own and do is a major source of argument among macroeconomists. It is not clear that both sets of records are of the same intrinsic interest and importance. One group of economists considers the national income accounts as the main item of interest—the changes in the balance sheets are merely consequences of income changes. The second group considers the balance sheet accounts as the main item of interest—the changes in the income accounts are merely consequences of balance sheet changes.

In a small way, the controversy is illustrated by Tiny Models 1 and 2. These reflect two basic positions held by economists. In one case, investment is held to be the main "factor" influencing the behavior of the economy. In the second, the quantity of money is held to be the main factor influencing the economy. Although these two theories are almost childishly simplified, they express this one central issue as to "what makes the economy tick." In more subtle and indirect forms, the two Tiny Models reappear in the most advanced and difficult macroeconomic theories.

Although the Tiny Models were stated as if they were quite unrelated, they are really interconnected, since changes in the quantity of money in Tiny Model 2 bring about changes in the quantity of plant desired. Changes in plant are changes in earning assets, and hence investment, by the reasoning shown in Chapter 2. Thus, investment is not really a factor (say the proponents of Tiny Model 2). It is a variable explainable by the quantity of money!

Or change the reasoning, just to show a fine impartiality. Tiny Model 2 has no debt account, so all increases in assets are increases in net worth. In Chapter 2, we associated increases in net worth with savings. Tiny Model 1 shows that if investment increases, savings will also increase; an increase in investment will therefore increase total assets, and hence should affect the quantity of money. Thus the quantity of money is not really a factor (say the proponents of Tiny Model 1). It is a variable explainable by the level of investment!

The views attributed in the last two paragraphs to the contestants are certainly not expressed as carefully or as precisely as they would be in an article written for professional economists. But like good caricatures, they are recognizable (if a bit unflattering) likenesses of two widely held opinions. If professional economists differ, beginners can hardly expect to be satisfied with any pat answer given them, but they should expect to be told clearly what the issue is.

The remainder of this book is concerned with assembling reasonably precise introductions to income economics and to balance sheet economics, and with explaining the relation between them. Fortunately, it is possible to set forth simple theories that explain the workings of pieces of the economy in the manner approved by one or more of the contestants, and readers will not find it hard to get some practice in analyzing the two views. When it comes to reconciling the two, it is not hard to state the issue and to explain why the conflict is still unresolved.

We turn first to economic theories about the national income, then to theories about the national balance sheets. Lastly, the relations between the two parts of the economy will be explored. It will first be useful to spell out just why Tiny Models 1 and 2 are unsatisfactory.

Tiny Model 1 states that the level of the national product depends on the level of consumer demand (F_C) and on investment (I). There is no explanation at all of how businesses decide how much to invest; they just do. Model 2 says that the wealth (total assets) of the community depends on business demand for plant and equipment (F_K) and on the quantity of money (M). There is no reason for the amount of money to be one number rather than another, and there is certainly no explanation of how money "enters the economy."

It is no criticism of either theory to say that some factors remain unexplained. Every theory leaves something unexplained. Only if we cease being men and become gods will we overcome this difficulty.

It is no criticism of either theory to say that some behavior implied by the theory is noneconomic. Thus, in saying that consumption depends in part on income, $C = aY + F_C$, we imply that part of consumption, in particular F_C, is determined by something outside the economy. (The economy consists of Y, C, I, and nothing else, and F_C does not depend on any of these.) All economic theories must recognize that *part* of human actions are not explained within the context of economic phenomena.

But one can reasonably object to the treatment of investment (I) as a factor. Tiny Model 1 says that businessmen decide on investment without even looking at what is going on around them. We might perfectly well grant that businesses invest partly because they think something *will* happen (and what *will happen* is not necessarily the same as what *is happening*). But one might guess that businesses would not last very long if their managers did not look to see what was happening around them.

Tiny Model 2 does not explain how money enters the economy. It does not relate money to income in any way. It suggests that "someone" (if so, who?) can simply change at will the amount of money.

Finally, one can object that the two models are completely independent of each other. Unless they are put together, economists are saying that: (a) There is no connection between the amount of plant and equipment and the gross national output. If there were, the variable K would have to appear in Tiny Model 1. (b) There is no connection between investment and the demand for plant, since I appears in Tiny Model 1, and K in Tiny Model 2. This is odd, because in Chapter 2, we pointed out that if an economy has K_0 plant today and if today's investment is I, the economy will have $(K_0 + I)$ plant tomorrow.

THEORY 1: MONEY, INTEREST, AND THE NATIONAL PRODUCT

In economic literature,[1] Theory 1 was the successor to first Tiny Model 1. It treats investment as something to be explained, not as an independent factor. It does so at the cost of making the amount of money an independent factor, as Tiny Model 2 did.

A new variable appears in Theory 1—the *rate of interest*. This variable is generally considered to be of fundamental importance in the operations of the economy.

[1] A nonlinear version of this theory is given in P. A. Samuelson, *Foundations of Economic Analysis*, Cambridge, Mass., 1948, p. 276. Samuelson says that this theory is essentially that of J. M. Keynes, *General Theory of Employment, Interest and Money*, London, 1935. We cannot be sure of this assertion because Keynes's book is, in many places, very obscure.

The rate of interest is a price, the price we pay when we borrow money, and the price we are paid when we lend money. Businesses borrow money in order to buy plant and equipment. In this respect, borrowing is associated with investing.[2] The rate of interest should influence investment decisions; and this influence is rather simply explained.

Suppose a business is deciding whether or not to build a new factory. The decision is based on a calculation which shows whether or not the proposed factory can be operated profitably. This calculation is like an income statement, but the figures in it are estimates about the future, not reports about the past. One of the costs to be estimated is the cost of borrowing enough to pay for the factory.

If the business had enough retained profits, it could pay for a new factory building without borrowing. However, if the operation of the new factory would not cover interest charges, the business would do better to lend its retained profits to someone else rather than to "lend them to itself" and build the factory.

The annual interest cost is obviously the cost of the new factory times the interest rate. The higher the interest rate at the time the calculation is made, the less profitable the operation of the factory will seem.

Imagine businesses as having collectively a long list of investment projects. At any moment, the going rate of interest rules out part of the list. The higher the rate of interest, the more projects will be ruled out. Theory 1 assumes that the demand for investment (the list of acceptable projects) is related to the interest rate (R):

$$I = dR + F_I$$

Here R is the rate of interest and $d < 0$. The factor F_I reminds us that the rate of interest is not the only thing affecting the demand for investment.

In Theory 1 households do not have a simple choice between consuming and saving. They may consume, hold cash, or lend to investors. If they lend, they receive interest in return; the higher the interest rate, the more consumers will presumably be willing to lend. Another way of saying this is: The higher the interest rate, the *less* households will consume, and the less cash they will wish to hold.[3] Thus, consumption is

$$C = aY + vL + bR + F_C$$

and the demand for money is

$$L = eR + F_L$$

[2] Of course, consumers also borrow whenever they buy on credit. This book does not consider consumer credit at all. All borrowing is done by businesses (or government).

[3] The original version of this theory, by Keynes, said that changes in interest rates do not affect consumption, but only the mixture of cash holding and lending in consumers' accounts. It is not really necessary to assert that consumption is not at all affected by the interest rate.

The symbol L stands for *liquidity*. Economic units are said to be liquid when they have enough cash for their needs. Obviously this is a fuzzy notion.[4] When we select this particular relation describing the demand for money, we give one precise interpretation of the liquidity concept.

It is not necessary to introduce a separate statement about the supply of savings to businesses by households. If this supply were denoted by S, then

$$S = Y - C - L$$

$$= (1 - a)Y - (b + e)R - vL - (F_C + F_L)$$

That is, $Y - C - L = S$ can be derived without difficulty from the other two statements.[5]

Theory 1 says that "the Government" is able to control the quantity of money. Thus L, the demand for money, must be equal to F_M, the amount of money provided by the authorities. F_M, then, is a factor.

The theory now contains five statements:

(1) The national product:

$$Y = C + I$$

(2) A consumption function:

$$C = aY + bR + vL + F_C$$

(3) A demand for investment:

$$I = dR + F_I$$

(4) A demand for money:

$$L = eR + F_L$$

(5) A supply of money F_M, which must equal demand:

$$L = F_M$$

Here the demand for money (4) and the supply of money are somewhat arbitrarily grafted on the tail of Tiny Model 1. This feature of Theory 1 reflects the fact that in 1935 the entire concept of reasoning on the basis of systematic national accounts was new. It has taken a number of years of discussion to clarify the structure of social accounting. Today, we would either include an entire balance sheet, or omit balance sheet accounts from the theory altogether.

[4] Do not confuse cash with profit. A business selling on credit may have large profits, but may be extremely short of cash because its assets consist mainly of accounts receivable. A business may be operating at a loss, but have large amounts of cash on hand.

[5] This particular formulation of consumer behavior is used because there are economists who maintain that consumer spending is more influenced by the size of consumer cash balances than by the size of the national income. These theorists, in effect, set $a = 0$.

As in Tiny Model 1 the *marginal propensity to save*, $(1 - a)$, is assumed greater than zero, so that part of every additional unit of income is saved.[6] The coefficient v is greater than zero: The more money there is, the more people spend and hence (other things being equal) the less they save. The rate of interest is an incentive to saving; therefore, $(b + e)$ must be negative. Holding cash means not lending money. Therefore holding cash means giving up income. An increase in the interest rate therefore reduces the amount of cash people want to hold. Thus e is negative, and it is natural to suppose that consumption will also be reduced by increases in the interest rate, so b is also negative.

This system of equations may be written in vector-matrix notation:

$$(\mathbf{0}, \mathbf{F_C}, \mathbf{F_I}, \mathbf{F_L}, \mathbf{F_M}) = (\mathbf{Y}, \mathbf{C}, \mathbf{I}, \mathbf{R}, \mathbf{L}) \begin{pmatrix} 1 & -a & 0 & 0 & 0 \\ -1 & 1 & 0 & 0 & 0 \\ -1 & 0 & 1 & 0 & 0 \\ 0 & -b & -d & -e & 0 \\ 0 & -v & 0 & 1 & 1 \end{pmatrix}$$

This system is block-triangular, and it contains Tiny Model 1 in the upper left. The inverse system may be shown to be

$$(\mathbf{0}, \mathbf{F_C}, \mathbf{F_I}, \mathbf{F_L}, \mathbf{F_M}) \begin{pmatrix} \frac{1}{1-a} & \frac{a}{1-a} & 0 & 0 & 0 \\ \frac{1}{1-a} & \frac{1}{1-a} & 0 & 0 & 0 \\ \frac{1}{1-a} & \frac{a}{1-a} & 1 & 0 & 0 \\ \frac{-b-d}{e(1-a)} & \frac{-b-da}{e(1-a)} & -\frac{d}{e} & -\frac{1}{e} & 0 \\ \frac{b+ev+d}{e(1-a)} & \frac{b+ev+da}{e(1-a)} & \frac{d}{e} & \frac{1}{e} & 1 \end{pmatrix} = (\mathbf{Y}, \mathbf{C}, \mathbf{I}, \mathbf{R}, \mathbf{L})$$

Table 4.1 interprets the elements of the inverse matrix. It will be seen that the arrangement of the table follows the structure of the matrix.[7]

In this theory, there are several elements that have been the object of

[6] In this context "savings" means "lending to business" because that part of income held as cash is accounted for by L.

[7] Readers will note, of course, that the first component of the factor vector is zero. This component will change if and only if the national product is redefined, so that output no longer is the sum of consumption and investment. Such a change would alter the structure of the theory, and is by hypothesis ruled out.

Table 4.1. The Implication of Theory 1

THE EFFECT OF A UNIT CHANGE IN	The Effect upon NATIONAL PRODUCT	CONSUMPTION	INVESTMENT	INTEREST RATE
The level of consumer demand (F_C)	$\frac{1}{1-a}$	$\frac{1}{1-a}$	0	0
Autonomous investment (F_I)	$\frac{1}{1-a}$	$\frac{a}{1-a}$	1	0
The level of liquidity demand F_L	$\frac{-b-d}{e(1-a)}$	$\frac{-b-da}{e(1-a)}$	$-\frac{d}{e}$	$-\frac{1}{e}$
The quantity of money (F_M)	$\frac{b+ev+d}{e(1-a)}$	$\frac{b+ev+da}{e(1-a)}$	$\frac{d}{e}$	$\frac{1}{e}$

Problem If $1 > a > 0$, $v > 0$, $b < 0$, $d < 0$, $e < 0$, is it possible to determine the signs of all these expressions?

debate among both professional economists and the public.

What use is money? The usual answer is that money is useful because it can be used to buy goods. If so, then the demand for money is different from the demand for other things. If I buy a steak, I buy it because I like steak. However, it seems that if I hold money, it is not because I like money. I like the things I can get with it. Why do I not get them instead of holding money? Well, I do not want them now.

One of the statements of Theory 1 says that people want to "buy" money. One consequence of this statement is that changes in the level of liquidity demand (F_L) and in the quantity of money (F_M) both affect the national product and its components.

Today this view seems harmless enough. In the 1930s it was revolutionary. The usual explanation of depression ran in terms of prices. Look at Tiny Model 3. If prices are *above* equilibrium levels, then the quantity demanded (q_D) will be less than the quantity supplied (q_s) so that there are unsalable goods. If the "goods" in question is labor, then there will be unemployment. The way to reduce unemployment is to cut wages, for then ($q_s - q_D$), which represents unemployment, will drop to zero.

The view in Theory 1 says something quite different: In a depression, there is unemployment because the demand for goods is so small that few people need be employed to make the goods. Instead of buying goods, people hoard money (that is, F_L is very large). An increase in F_L automatically reduces both consumption and investment. But it can be offset if there is a sufficient *increase* in the quantity of money.

The older theory prescribed a *decrease* in the money supply. This prescription followed from what is called the *quantity theory of money*, which related the price level to the quantity of money. The theory used the formula $MV = PQ$, where M is the quantity of money, V is a constant called *velocity*, P is the price level, and Q is the level of output.[8] If the trouble in a depression is that there are unsold goods, and if there are unsold goods because prices are too high, then a decrease in the money supply (on this formula) would *lower* prices and therefore eliminate unemployment.[9]

Problem Suppose that all the factors in the system are given. What is the effect on the values of the variables if there is an increase in a? In v? In b? In d? In e?

Problem A somewhat simpler theory than Theory 1 states

$$Y = C + I$$
$$C = aY + bR + F_C$$
$$I = dR + F_I$$

In this theory the rate of interest (R) appears as a factor. Suppose R can be controlled by "the government." Is it possible that whatever the decrease in autonomous investment (F_I) is, "the government" can prevent the national income from falling by forcing down the interest rate?

Problem Discuss the connection between the views given in Theory 1 and the views in the preceding problem.

THEORY 2: GOVERNMENT AND THE NATIONAL PRODUCT

The government has all sorts of complicated effects on the economy. Business cannot be carried on without laws and courts (one of whose roles is to interpret and enforce contracts). In some economies (as in the United States), government has encouraged businesses to compete with each other; in other cases (as in most of Europe) governments have encouraged businesses not to compete, but to divide markets by agreement, to fix prices, and so on. There is no simple way even to list all the ways in which legal and political arrangements affect the economy, and this book will not even try to. It will discuss a few matters in detail.

In this book, the government has two functions: It buys goods and it collects taxes. As a buyer of goods, it enters into the national product, the definition of which now becomes

$$Y = C + I + G$$

Consumption (C) and investment (I) are thus joined by government spend-

[8] This theory is mentioned again in the first part of Chapter 6.

[9] This brief summary does not do justice to the formula or to the views of its modern adherents (who are still numerous). But it is not an unreasonable view of one side of the debate in the 1930s. The formula in this paragraph will reappear in Chapter 6.

ing (G). The government raises income from taxes (T), and it has a surplus or deficit given by $(G - T)$. It is natural to ask how the government can pay for the goods it buys if it does not have enough tax revenue. The present theory does not answer this question, but two informal suggestions can be made. First, the government can print paper money; second, it can sell bonds. Both money and bonds, of course, are part of the assets (wealth) of the community, and therefore they do not enter explicitly into the income accounts. The reader must wait for Theory 6, which imbeds the income theory given here into a more comprehensive system.

Tax revenue is assumed to be described by the relation

$$T = tY + F_T$$

This statement says that when the national product increases, tax revenue also increases, and t is taken to be positive. It will also be assumed that t is less than 1. That is, when income increases, not all of the increase goes to the government.

The reasoning behind this statement is simple. The two main sources of government revenue in all civilized countries are called *income taxes* and *excise taxes*. An income tax is collected from people (or businesses) on the basis of their incomes: The more each person earns, the more tax he pays, and the more income the community earns, the more taxes it pays.[10] Excise taxes are taxes levied on the sale of particular products, such as gasoline, tobacco, and liquor—many governments depend heavily on such taxes. These tax collections presumably depend on income because when consumers have more income, they buy more of the taxed goods and hence pay more taxes. The relation between excise taxes and income is obviously much trickier than that given here, but this particular formulation probably contains an important part of the connection.

Not all taxes are related to income. State and local governments in the United States have traditionally depended on taxes on property (land and buildings, in particular). This sort of tax does not vary automatically with income. For this reason a term F_T enters into the statement about taxes.

Tiny Model 1 stated the following about consumption:

$$C = aY + F_C$$

That means consumption depends on total income. But if consumers are liable to an income tax, their spending must depend on income *after* tax, rather than total income. In the present theory, the simplest way of taking this important fact into account is to say that:

$$C = a(Y - T) + F_C$$

[10] This statement is a typical macroeconomic exaggeration. Imagine that high-income groups are subject to a high tax and low-income groups to a low tax. It is then arithmetically possible in some year for low-income groups to get increased incomes, and high-income groups to get reduced incomes in such a way that total income rises and tax payments fall. The reader can easily construct an example of this sort. Since this book aims at simplicity, we will not go into this sort of complication.

For the moment, assume that investment and government spending are independent of the rest of the system. That is, they are factors rather than variables:

$$I = F_I$$
$$G = F_G$$

Now for the mechanics of obtaining the factor-into-variable mapping. The discussion thus far gives us the variable-into-factor mapping:

$$(\mathbf{0}, \mathbf{F_C}, \mathbf{F_T}, \mathbf{F_G}, \mathbf{F_I}) = (\mathbf{Y}, \mathbf{C}, \mathbf{T}, \mathbf{G}, \mathbf{I}) \begin{pmatrix} 1 & -a & -t & 0 & 0 \\ -1 & 1 & 0 & 0 & 0 \\ 0 & a & 1 & 0 & 0 \\ -1 & 0 & 0 & 1 & 0 \\ -1 & 0 & 0 & 0 & 1 \end{pmatrix}$$

This matrix contains Tiny Model 1 in its upper left corner:

$$\begin{pmatrix} 1 & -a \\ -1 & 1 \end{pmatrix}$$

and it is block-triangular, since there is a 3×2 block of zeros in the upper right. The inverse of the matrix may be shown to be

$$\begin{pmatrix} 1 & -a & -t & 0 & 0 \\ -1 & 1 & 0 & 0 & 0 \\ 0 & a & 1 & 0 & 0 \\ -1 & 0 & 0 & 1 & 0 \\ -1 & 0 & 0 & 0 & 1 \end{pmatrix}^{-1}$$

$$= \begin{pmatrix} \frac{1}{1-a(1-t)} & \frac{a(1-t)}{1-a(1-t)} & \frac{t}{1-a(1-t)} & 0 & 0 \\ \frac{1}{1-a(1-t)} & \frac{1}{1-a(1-t)} & \frac{t}{1-a(1-t)} & 0 & 0 \\ \frac{-a}{1-a(1-t)} & \frac{-a}{1-a(1-t)} & \frac{1-a}{1-a(1-t)} & 0 & 0 \\ \frac{1}{1-a(1-t)} & \frac{a(1-t)}{1-a(1-t)} & \frac{t}{1-a(1-t)} & 1 & 0 \\ \frac{1}{1-a(1-t)} & \frac{a(1-t)}{1-a(1-t)} & \frac{t}{1-a(1-t)} & 0 & 1 \end{pmatrix}$$

Table 4.2. The Implications of Theory 2

THE EFFECT OF A UNIT CHANGE IN	The Effect of a Unit Change upon NATIONAL PRODUCT	CONSUMPTION	TAX REVENUE
F_C: (Consumer demand)	$\frac{1}{1 - a(1 - t)}$	$\frac{1}{1 - a(1 - t)}$	$\frac{t}{1 - a(1 - t)}$
F_T: (Property taxes)	$\frac{-a}{1 - a(1 - t)}$	$\frac{-a}{1 - a(1 - t)}$	$\frac{1 - a}{1 - a(1 - t)}$
F_G: (Government spending)	$\frac{1}{1 - a(1 - t)}$	$\frac{a(1 - t)}{1 - a(1 - t)}$	$\frac{t}{1 - a(1 - t)}$
F_I: (Investment)	$\frac{1}{1 - a(1 - t)}$	$\frac{a(1 - t)}{1 - a(1 - t)}$	$\frac{t}{1 - a(1 - t)}$

The interpretation of the inverse matrix is given by Table 4.2.

Theory 2 has an intimate connection with Tiny Model 1. The *investment multiplier* in the latter was $1/(1 - a)$, in this case it is $1/[1 - a(1 - t)]$. In the first case, it was said that if consumers received an additional dollar of income, they consumed an additional a, so that they *save* $(1 - a)$, which appears in the denominator.

In Theory 2, when consumers receive an additional dollar of income, they pay t in additional taxes. Therefore they have $(1 - t)$ left, and of this they spend $a(1 - t)$. Consequently, for every additional dollar of income *before* taxes, savings increase by $[1 - a(1 - t)]$, that is, by exactly the denominator of the investment multiplier. In other words, the two theories are very much the same.

Problem Suppose F_T (property taxes) are altered in such a way that when government spending increases by \$1.00, total tax collections also increase by \$1.00. What is the effect of this coordinated change in the budget on the national product and on consumption?

Historical Note

The last two lines of Table 4.2 are the same. That is, in this theory, a dollar's change in investment has the same effect throughout the economy as a dollar's change in government spending. This theory is known in the popular press as "Keynesian," although economists will be far more inclined to consider Theory 1 as Keynesian. Keynes was more interested in money than in government spending and taxation.

Theory 2 represents a rationalization of a major political discovery, which, for thirty years, had a profound effect on American life. In 1929, the United States entered a period of massive depression. By 1932, over one quarter of the labor force was unemployed, and business conditions were in all respects worse than they ever have been (before *or* since). In those days, everyone believed that government deficits were in general undesirable, although no theory of any consequence existed that could be stated as precisely (say) as Table 4.2. Consequently, in the elections of 1932, both Republicans and Democrats advocated reduced government spending, which, if Table 4.2 is valid, means that they both advocated policies that would make the depression worse.

Of course, the Democrats won the election, because the electorate blamed President Hoover either for causing the depression or for massive indifference to its consequences. We would now consider this verdict unfair. No convincing explanation has ever been given for the violence of this depression, but it affected the entire world, and no country was able to combat it successfully for a long time except by using Nazi or Communist methods.

When President Roosevelt came into office, there were so many unemployed that mass starvation seemed to threaten. Disregarding the professional advice of economists (and following that of politicians and social workers), Roosevelt began providing relief to the unemployed. Everyone expected business conditions to get worse, because of the increased government deficit. Lo and behold! It turned out that if the government gave money to the unemployed, they promptly spent it. When they spent it, business earned income, and when business received more income it hired more people, and unemployment fell. To the surprise of economists, business conditions improved considerably in 1933–1934.

The entire development of macroeconomics has been profoundly influenced by these shocking events. At the time, they dumbfounded the experts. Theory 2 gives the easy explanation of what happened. We should *not*, of course, conclude that Theory 2 is the *true* explanation of this period. It would require considerable historical analysis to determine that matter. But it is a fact that Theory 2 was developed in order to explain the depression of 1929–1932 and the partial recovery of 1933–1936.

It is difficult for students in the late 1960s to appreciate the enormous emotional content which Theory 2 has for economists of their parents' age. In purely professional terms, economists say that this theory was the first explanation offered for the depression of the 1930s, and the principal remedy for it which seemed to be available at the time. And of course, the depression itself was as important a topic of popular concern in the 1930s as Outer Space, the Hydrogen Bomb, and Communist China, together, are in the late 1960s.

Theory 3 will formulate a problem concerning the effect of government on the economy. If the answer to this problem were known, then an issue that can now only be debated about could be resolved. It is a precise statement (in a very simple form) of an economic issue which divides political liberals from political conservatives, and as such is of interest outside the narrow circle of professional economists.

THEORY 3: GOVERNMENT AND INVESTMENT

Most undergraduates who take economics courses do not intend to become professional economists, but all will become voters. Therefore, most teachers of undergraduate economics courses feel that part of their role is to help their students to become intelligent voters. Some of these teachers feel that if their students are to be intelligent voters, they must adopt the political views of their professors. But the more responsible teachers recognize that economists themselves have quite varied political opinions; and therefore most political parties (and factions within political parties) will be able to find some supporters among professional economists. Whatever political group one considers, its views on economic questions can certainly be formulated, in most cases, in a literate fashion. Professional economists, as partisans, can keep their political friends from saying unsound things, and sometimes even (if these friends are in power) dissuade them from doing foolish things.

Political questions arise in part because different political groups want different things. In such cases, any economist can, in principle, be employed by any political group. One can imagine (in the extreme) an economist, in wartime, acting as consultant to both warring powers on tax policy. It is unlikely, of course, that any economist would be trusted by both parties; if he were, it is unlikely that he would be so indifferent to the outcome of the war that he would be willing to work for both sides. As a professional matter, of course, he could do so.

But political questions arise, in part, because there is a variety of opinion on the truth of some matter, and no scientific answer is yet possible. In cases such as this, political disagreement is associated with professional disagreement. One would hope that if professional economists resolve the issue conclusively, the political factions would be able to recognize that an answer exists, so that controversy is unnecessary.

One example of a problem that has been resolved has to do with "bimetallism." In the nineteenth century and before, money consisted largely of metal coin. Some countries used gold coin, others used silver coin. A few, including the United States, had both kinds. Countries that wished to use both sorts of coin had to decide whether or not to keep the prices of the two kinds stable relative to each other. This decision involved a dilemma: If the relative prices of the two kinds of money were fixed, then people tended to hoard one kind and only the other would remain in general use; if prices were not fixed, both remained in use, but grave uncertainty arose in the conduct of business, for it was in principle necessary in each contract to specify what kind of money was to be used. In the late 1800s there was important political agitation on the question of maintaining both kinds of coin; it reached its peak in the presidential election of 1896, when McKinley beat Bryan in a campaign largely concerned with monetary issues.

It is most unlikely that this issue could be taken seriously today. Professional economists would now say that Bryan's sound argument was that the quantity of money should be increased as a means of increasing incomes (particularly for farmers), a proposition defensible in terms of the theories given here; but that increases in the quantity of money can be more readily achieved through the formation and utilization of a central bank (see Chapter 6) rather than by making silver coins. We should now say that McKinley's sound argument was that unless care is taken to avoid undue increase in the amount of money, prices will indeed tend to rise, but there may be better ways of stabilizing the amount of money than by insisting on the use of gold coins. Professional economists today would urge both McKinley and Bryan to concentrate on the central question—how large should the money supply be if it is to stabilize income and prices, rather than on the issue of gold and silver coinage. Political leaders of all persuasions now get better advice than formerly, so that certain controversies have simply disappeared. Of course, the connection between money and economic activity is still full of unsolved issues.

The great political issue that was resolved in principle in the 1930s was whether increases in government spending might affect the level of the national product. That issue is solved in Theory 2. If one theory can be constructed to show how *some* effect is produced by changes in government spending, others can presumably be constructed to show how other effects might come about. The intelligent citizen, whatever his political beliefs, has no reason to doubt the *logical* consistency of Theory 2. The world, of course, may or may not behave in the way depicted by this theory.

It is useful to replace Theory 2 by a theory that differs from it in the following respect: Investment will be taken to depend partly on other variables in the system, instead of being completely "outside" the system. This theory, then, has something in common with Theory 1, in which the interest rate was introduced as a variable affecting investment. However, this time no new variables will be introduced. The number of nonzero elements in the matrix of Theory 3 will be reduced by replacing the relation $I = F_I$ with the relation:

$$I = cC + gT + hG + F_I$$

connecting investment with consumption, taxes, and government spending. Consequently Theory 3, written out in full, is

$$(\mathbf{0}, \mathbf{F_C}, \mathbf{F_T}, \mathbf{F_G}, \mathbf{F_I}) = (\mathbf{Y}, \mathbf{C}, \mathbf{T}, \mathbf{G}, \mathbf{I}) \begin{pmatrix} 1 & -a & -t & 0 & 0 \\ -1 & 1 & 0 & 0 & -c \\ 0 & a & 1 & 0 & -g \\ -1 & 0 & 0 & 1 & -h \\ -1 & 0 & 0 & 0 & 1 \end{pmatrix}$$

The first four columns of the matrix of Theories 3 and 4 are the same, only the last column is changed.

Why write such a theory? The point is that with this theory we can comment usefully on a political controversy over government spending. This controversy is one step higher than the controversy over Theory 2. It recognizes that government spending affects the national income; and, in fact, Theory 2 emerges as a special case of Theory 3 (set $c = g = h = 0$). Thus, when Theory 2 is generalized, an interesting problem is obtained.

Investment, in a private enterprise economy, takes place whenever business *expects* to make a profit from operating the proposed facility. Expectations pertain to the future, not to the present. One obtains an expectation about the future, partly by looking at the present, partly by looking at the past, and partly by completely extraneous means.[11]

The present theory states that consumption affects investment and, in particular, $c \geq 0$. The mechanism posited is the following: The more consumption there is today, the more business expects there will be tomorrow. The larger the size of the expected market, the more plant and equipment business will decide it needs, so the more investment there will be.[12]

The present theory also states that taxes affect investment, and in particular, $g \leq 0$. An increase in tax payments reduces investment. The justification of this view would be just like the explanation of why increases in the interest rate reduce investment. That is, the firm estimates the capacity and hence the sales to be obtained from the new facility and the cost of operating the facility. If taxes rise, the expected cost of the new facility rises,

[11] Economists call factors unrelated to the economy *psychological*, and they mean by this statement *irrational*. No slur on psychologists is intended.

[12] Some economists make investment depend on the *change* in consumption, not the amount of consumption, as here. This assumption would follow, if, in this theory, balance sheet items were present, and if the demand for *plant* depended on the *amount* of consumption. Then investment (the change in plant) would depend on the change in consumption. This hypothesis is called the *accelerator* hypothesis. It is interesting but more difficult than anything we use here.

and expected profits fall. Any increase in taxes might be expected, then, to reduce investment.[13]

Finally, the present theory states that government spending affects investment. But there are two widely different views about the nature of the effect. Both views can be documented for individual industries.

(1) Political conservatives say that $h < 0$, for two reasons. The first is that government spending may compete with business. *Example*: If the government builds a hydroelectric dam on the Wabash River, this project will cause private public utilities *not* to build such plants on the Wabash. More generally, if business sees that government spending is rising, it infers that ultimately the business sector of the economy will be forced to contract. Thus, even if the dam did not directly replace a private project, it would cause reductions in investment in general.
(2) Political liberals say that $h > 0$ for two reasons. First, government spending leads directly to business investment. *Example*: If the government builds a hydroelectric dam on the Wabash River, the project will cause nearby businesses to expand. The workers on the building project must be fed, clothed, lodged, and entertained. Later, the dam will attract power-using firms into the area, and so on. More generally, if business sees that government spending is rising, it infers that it will receive increased orders, both from the government and from government employees; to meet this increase in orders, business therefore invests more.

Both of these views are plausible. We need only read what businessmen say about government in the annual reports of corporations, or in the financial newspapers, to be aware that many of them seem to be very suspicious indeed of government. If they do not lie about their true sentiments, something like the "conservative investment function" ($h < 0$) is defensible. On the other hand, we need only look at cities such as Oak Ridge, Tennessee, Groton, Connecticut, San Diego, California, or Seattle, Washington to see cases where government spending (on atomic energy, submarines, and the "aerospace" industries) have had indirect effects on housing construction and all sorts of business investments. If this evidence is not completely misleading, something like the "liberal investment function" ($h > 0$) is defensible.

In fact, if both hypotheses are plausible, and if there is evidence in favor of both, the only question would be, "Which is the more important"? In this problem, the symbol h would be regarded as a sum of two influences:

[13] To the extent that business can "pass taxes on" and make its customers or stockholders pay them, this argument is weakened. At this point we are not saying whether g is close to zero, or whether investment is greatly affected by taxes. The point is that it is implausible that increased taxes should *increase* investment.

$h = h_C + h_L$, and one would seek to evaluate relative magnitudes. We will not be concerned with this problem here. The point is, simply, that the answer to the problem is one in applied economics (is h a positive or a negative number in the conditions of country A in year Y?) and not merely one for speech-makers to emote about.

Part of investment does not depend on the other variables in the system. Denoted by F_I, it is called *autonomous* investment in traditional terminology. The rest of investment, $I - F_I$, is called *induced*, because it depends on the other variables in the system. F_I, of course, is a factor.

In the present state of our knowledge, political contestants try to resolve the argument by standing nose-to-nose and shouting "$h > 0$!" or "$h < 0$!" at each other. This may seem silly to some bystanders, because a question of fact is involved. Why don't these people find out where the truth lies? Two answers to this question may be given: (1) Some efforts have been made, but (as we shall see in the last chapter), it is at best not easy to answer such questions. (2) Although the question is important, people with strong political views do not want to try too hard for an answer; they are afraid they may be wrong. Here is a case where the interested reader may be invited to devise a way of finding the truth about this argument. The argument itself is getting nowhere.

Why should it matter whether h is greater than, or less than, zero? To answer this question, we must invert the matrix so as to obtain the factor-into-variable mapping. The inverse of the matrix to Theory 3 is

$$\begin{pmatrix} 1 & -a & -t & 0 & 0 \\ -1 & 1 & 0 & 0 & -c \\ 0 & a & 1 & 0 & -g \\ -1 & 0 & 0 & 1 & -h \\ -1 & 0 & 0 & 0 & 1 \end{pmatrix}^{-1}$$

$$= \begin{pmatrix} \frac{1}{D} & \frac{a(1-t)}{D} & \frac{t}{D} & 0 & \frac{ca(1-t)+gt}{D} \\ \frac{1+c}{D} & \frac{1-gt}{D} & \frac{t(1+c)}{D} & 0 & \frac{c+gt}{D} \\ \frac{g-a(1+c)}{D} & \frac{-a(1-g)}{D} & \frac{1-a(1+c)}{D} & 0 & \frac{-ca(1-g)+g(1-a(1+c))}{D} \\ \frac{1+h}{D} & \frac{a(1-t)(1+h)}{D} & \frac{t(1+h)}{D} & 1 & \frac{a(h-c)(1-t)-h-gt}{D} \\ \frac{1}{D} & \frac{a(1-t)}{D} & \frac{t}{D} & 0 & \frac{1-a(1-t)}{D} \end{pmatrix}$$

where $D = (1 - gt) - a(1 - t)(1 + c)$.

Table 4.3 is the interpretation given to the elements of the inverse matrix just calculated. Let us note that $1/D$ measures the effect of increased autonomous investment on the national product, and is thus the investment multiplier. In Tiny Model 1, the corresponding multiplier was $1/(1 - a)$. The quantity D may be interpreted as follows:

The quantity a represents the amount spent from a unit increase in income after taxes; t is the tax rate. Hence $a(1 - t)$ represents the change in consumption from a unit increase in income *before* taxes; $a(1 - t)(1 + c)$ adjusts this change for the increase in investment associated with the change in consumption just mentioned. That is, the final term of D represents a change in consumption. Then, $(1 - gt)$ measures the net increase in income after taxes. Thus D represents the amount of saving per unit of additional income; it is one dollar income minus taxes on one dollar additional income minus spending generated by 1 dollar additional income. This multiplier is more difficult than the earlier multipliers, because Theory 3 involves more internal connections than the earlier theories.

Note that in this theory, if investment increases by one dollar, the national product goes *up* by $1/D$. We say "up" because we suppose that at a higher level of income, the community saves more ($D > 0$).[14] On the other hand, an increase in government spending increases the national product by $(1 + h)/D$.

Conclusion: If the political conservatives are right, and h is between 0 and -1, then if the government wished to compensate for a decline of one dollar in autonomous business investment, it would have to increase spending by more than one dollar.

If an extreme conservative view is right, and $h < -1$, then an increase of one dollar in government spending decreases investment by more than one dollar. In this case, $(1 + h)/D$ is negative. To offset a decline in autonomous investment, then the government should *reduce* spending, so as to stimulate investment and hence increase the national product. On the other hand, in wartime, when resources are scarce, and the government wishes to reduce civilian purchasing power, it should (in this view) *increase* its spending so as to contract the civilian sector.

If the political liberals are right, h is positive; an increase of one dollar in government spending would more than offset a decline of one dollar in autonomous investment. On the other hand, in wartime, on this argument, a reduction in government spending (presumably nonmilitary) would be more effective in restricting civilian purchasing power than an equal restriction in business investment.

No convincing answers have been given by economists to the question "what is the numerical value of h?" Obviously, if such answers could be

[14] Note that $D = 1 - a(1 + c) + t(a + ac - g)$. If $g < 0$ (taxes reduce investment), the last term is positive. Indeed, the smaller g is (the more taxes reduce investment), the greater D is. That is, the less $1/D$ is, the less investment increases the national product.

Table 4.3. The Implications of Theory 3

THE EFFECT OF A UNIT CHANGE IN	*The Effect of a Unit Change upon*			
	NATIONAL PRODUCT	CONSUMPTION	TAXES	INVESTMENT
F_C: (The level of consumption)	$\frac{1 + c}{D}$	$\frac{1 - gt}{D}$	$\frac{t(1 + c)}{D}$	$\frac{c + gt}{D}$
F_T: (Property taxes)	$\frac{g - a(1 + c)}{D}$	$\frac{-a(1 - g)}{D}$	$\frac{1 - a(1 + c)}{D}$	$\frac{-ca(1 - g) + g(1 - a(1 + c))}{D}$
F_G: (Government spending)	$\frac{1 + h}{D}$	$\frac{a(1 - t)(1 + h)}{D}$	$\frac{t(1 + h)}{D}$	$\frac{a(h - c)(1 - t) - h - gt}{D}$
F_I: (Autonomous investment)	$\frac{1}{D}$	$\frac{a(1 - t)}{D}$	$\frac{t}{D}$	$\frac{1 - a(1 - t)}{D}$

given, there would be one less controversy. In passing, let us observe that even if we knew for sure that in some particular year, h had some particular numerical value, there would be no certainty that the next year h would remain unchanged. For h, like all the other symbols used in one of these theories, is a way of summarizing people's behavior. There is a great deal we do not know about people, including how changeable they are.

Problem Suppose F_T (property taxes) are altered in such a way that when government spending increases by one dollar, total tax collections also increase by one dollar. What is the effect of this coordinated change in the budget on the national product and on consumption? Compare the answer you gave to this identical question in connection with Theory 3. Why is your answer now different?

5

MONEY AND THE ECONOMY

MONEY AND BALANCE SHEET ECONOMICS

In Chapter 2, we pointed out that the national income and the national balance sheet are the basic records of the economy. Tiny Models 1 and 2 in Chapter 3 were the analytical introduction to these respective documents. After a discussion, in Chapter 4 on income determination, we come to a chapter on money. Money is only a component of balance sheets. Why discuss only a part, rather than the whole?

In fact, the following discussion will deal with balance sheets. Each theory in Chapter 4 contained a definition of the national income, and each theory in this chapter will contain one or more balance sheets. The chapter is named *Money*, because money is considered the most significant, interesting, and puzzling part of the balance sheet, from the analytical point of view. For this reason, the macroeconomics dealing with national balance sheets is usually called *monetary*. Everyone knows that banks deal with money, and it is not surprising to find *money* and *banking* linked together (for instance, in the names of college courses).

In recent years, it has increasingly been recognized that there is indeed a fine line between banking and nonbanking institutions. The term *financial intermediaries* is sometimes used to describe things that are almost-banks, or semi-banks.[1] The term *capital markets* is used to describe that part of the economy populated by financial intermediaries and their customers. The

[1] Savings banks, mutual savings institutions, savings and loan associations, investment banks, and insurance companies all have something in common with the *commercial banks* dealt with in this chapter.

theories in this chapter are simple explanations of the operations of the banks and capital markets.

The importance of the banks and financial intermediaries lies in their ability to provide purchasing power to their customers. Banks, in fact, "create" money, a fact that beginning students find extremely hard to believe. But our readers are entitled to an explanation. In Theory 1, money simply "appeared" from nowhere, and was poured into the economy from somewhere, causing the national product to change. Was this assertion nonsense? Let us see how such a thing can happen.

SOMETHING UNBELIEVABLE BUT TRUE

Imagine the quiet town of Podunk, whose inhabitants live according to the customs traditional to small towns: Half the town earns its living taking in the laundry of the other half; and the other half sells catnip to the first half. The money of Podunk consists of paper money, $1.00 bills containing the inscription, "One dollar. This note is legal tender for all debts, public and private." [2]

Mr. Smith of Podunk, after participating in a television program in the Big City, returns home with a suitcase containing 64,000 dollar bills. He decides to open a bank, The First National Bank of Podunk, which will have checking accounts. The essence of a checking account is that any holder of the account may *demand* dollar bills up to the amount of his account, and the bank must *on demand* (that is, instantly), give him his money. At this point (disregarding the legal formalities that go with setting up banks in real life), Mr. Smith's bank has cash assets of $64,000 and net worth (common stock) of $64,000.

The Smiths and the Joneses are bitter rivals in town society, and Mr. Jones is not to be outdone. So he rips up his mattress, takes out $36,000 in dollar bills he has sewn into it, and creates his bank, The Last National Bank of Podunk, which thus has cash assets of $36,000 and net worth (common stock) of $36,000.

Banks are businesses, and earn their income by making loans. On Monday morning, Mr. White enters the First National Bank to borrow $20,000 to buy a house from Mr. Green. He signs an IOU and emerges with $20,000 in one dollar bills, and buys his house. Mr. Green decides it would be unsafe to keep the cash at home, so he deposits the $20,000 in an account with the Last National Bank. Now the balance sheets of the banks are as follows:

[2] Read the small print on a dollar bill. This statement means that the courts may require you to pay your debt in such money, and that paying any debt in such money is good enough to satisfy any court.

First National Bank		Last National Bank	
Cash, 44,000	Net worth, 64,000	Cash, 56,000	Green account, 20,000
White loan, 20,000			Net worth, 36,000

The Green account is a liability of the bank. The bank *owes* Mr. Green $20,000 and it promises to give it to him any time he wants it. Mr. Green can pay his bills by check. That is, the account is money to Mr. Green.

Next Mr. Brown enters the Last National Bank and borrows $20,000 to buy a house from Mr. Black. He signs an IOU and takes 20,000 dollar bills to Mr. Black, who deposits them in an account in the First National Bank. Then the bank balance sheets are:

First National Bank		Last National Bank	
Cash, 64,000	Black account, 20,000	Cash, 36,000	Green account, 20,000
White loan, 20,000	Net worth, 64,000	Brown loan, 20,000	Net worth, 36,000

Notice several things:

(1) The First National Bank still has $64,000 in one dollar bills.
(2) The Last National Bank still has $36,000 in one dollar bills.
(3) Mr. Black and Mr. Green have $20,000 apiece in the bank, which they received from the sale of their houses. This sum is real money; they can buy goods and pay bills with it. It is not, however, money that was "brought into" a bank in any ordinary sense of the word. To be brought in, it would have to have been deposited in some dollar bills *other than* the $64,000 used by Mr. Smith or the $36,000 used by Mr. Jones to start their banks. These were the only dollar bills used.

Readers who doubt this conclusion may work the process in reverse. Suppose Mr. Brown owns the Indomitable Catnip Company. Mr. Green buys $1,000 of catnip from him, paying by check, and Mr. Brown uses the check to repay part of his debt to the bank. Then the balance sheet of the First National Bank is the same, while that of the Last National Bank becomes:

Last National Bank	
Cash, 36,000	Green account, 19,000
Brown loan, 19,000	Net worth, 36,000

Bank loans and checking accounts both declined $1,000, and there is less money in Podunk than formerly.

The consolidated (that is, combined) balance sheets of this banking system, immediately before Mr. Brown repaid his loan, would show:

Consolidated Balance Sheet

Cash,	100,000	Deposits,	40,000
Loans,	40,000	Net worth,	100,000

There was no reason for the banks to cease making loans. In American conditions, the loans of banks[3] are ordinarily seven or eight times as large as cash (called *reserves*; and net worth is only a few percent of deposits). Thus $100,000 of reserves would produce a consolidated balance sheet more like this:

Consolidated Balance Sheet

Reserves,	100,000	Deposits,	700,000
Loans,	650,000	Net worth,	50,000

A second element of unreality in our story has been the statement that the reserves of the banks consisted of dollar bills. Actually, the reserves of the banks consist mainly of bank accounts, which are kept in special "banks for banks"—the *Federal Reserve Banks.* Only if a bank needs dollar bills today does it have dollar bills. To get them, it cashes a check on its *reserve account* (its account with Federal Reserve). Federal Reserve *always* has enough dollar bills because it prints them. (If you do not believe this statement, look at the top line on a piece of paper money.)

The Federal Reserve System[4] replaces certain elements of the banking system just described. Thus it takes care of the movement of reserves from bank to bank. Suppose Mr. Black pays Mr. Green $1,000. In the context given above, Mr. Green would go to Mr. Black's bank, cash the check, take the dollar bills to his own bank, and deposit them. Thus the reserves of the First National Bank go down $1,000 and those of the Last National Bank go up by $1,000 because Mr. Black has paid Mr. Green.

When there is a central bank, like the Federal Reserve System, then if Mr. Green deposits Mr. Black's check, the Last National Bank (which owns

[3] Actually banks also own large amounts of government and other bonds, which are termed "investments." For simplicity, they are ignored here.

[4] There are twelve regional banks that actually do the day-to-day business of the system. These banks do what they are told to do by the Board of Governors of the Federal Reserve System, which is an independent government agency in Washington, D.C. "Government agency" means that the Governors, (members of the Board) are appointed by the President of the United States with the advice and consent of the Senate. "Independent" means that once the President has appointed a Governor, he cannot remove him or tell him what to do; moreover, Congress has no direct control over the Board (unless it changes the basic law). The Federal Reserve System makes a profit and does not have to ask Congress for money. Almost all other government agencies must.

the check) deposits the check in its reserve account. This means that Federal Reserve acquires the check; it returns it to the First National Bank, and charges it against the reserve account. Then the First National Bank charges the check against Mr. Black's account. In each case, the bank in question hands over a check to a depositor. That is, it gives up an asset (checks, after all, are money), and reduces correspondingly its debts to its depositors. This check-clearing operation assures a technically efficient way of handling payments by check; these payments automatically move reserves among individual banks.

Whenever bank lending increases, the quantity of bank deposits (money) increases. However, when individual banks make loans, these loans do not necessarily affect the lending bank's deposits; instead, each loan tends to draw down the lender's reserves. Each loan by a given bank tends to increase the deposits of all other banks in the system, and the mechanism is fundamentally that described here.

TINY MODEL 4: THE BANKING SYSTEM

Tiny Model 2 has a banking interpretation. If we disregard the net worth of banks,[5] the balance sheet of the banking system may be described as:

$$M = R + L$$

That is, deposits (M) make up the liabilities side of the balance sheet, while reserves (R) and loans (L) make up the assets.

One function of the Federal Reserve System is to force the banks to maintain cash balances. In banking systems that are not regulated, there is a strong incentive for banks to overexpand credit (that is, to keep too little cash). The reason is that loans produce income for the banks in the form of interest, while cash does not. The reserve requirements laid down by Federal Reserve are stated in terms of deposits: Reserves *must* be at least r percent of deposits. Banks may, of course, have *excess* reserves (that is, reserves in excess of requirements), which may be denoted F_R. Thus,

$$R = rM + F_R$$

divides total reserves into *required* reserves (rM) and *excess* reserves (F_R). It follows that loans depend on excess reserves and the reserve ratio r:

$$L = M - R = (1 - r)M - F_R$$

[5] Net worth of banks is only a few percent of their balance sheet totals. The net worth accounts of banks tend to be stable, and only in rather specialized problems does this account play any role. Therefore, the accounts, for present purposes, are omitted from the theory.

Consequently,

$$(\mathbf{R}, -\mathbf{F_R}) = (\mathbf{M}, \mathbf{L}) \begin{pmatrix} 1 & (1-r) \\ -1 & -1 \end{pmatrix}$$

That is,

$$(\mathbf{M}, \mathbf{L}) = (\mathbf{R}, -\mathbf{F_R}) \begin{pmatrix} \frac{1}{r} & \frac{1-r}{r} \\ -\frac{1}{r} & -\frac{1}{r} \end{pmatrix}$$

Thus, the quantity of money (M) and of bank loans (L) can be explained by the level of bank reserves (R) and by the excess reserves (F_R) desired by the banks; and of course by the reserve ratio (r) set by Federal Reserve. Obviously F_R is something that the banks (collectively) decide upon. Bank reserves are beyond their control. It will now be shown that Federal Reserve can determine bank reserves (with certain restrictions).

THEORY 4: A PURE BANKING THEORY

The Federal Reserve System is a collection of banks. Their deposits consist of the reserves (cash assets) of the private banks. It is natural to consider a very simple theory of the relation between the Federal Reserve System and the private banks. Such a theory involves the specification of balance sheets in both kinds of banks. These are assumed to be of the following form[6]:

FEDERAL RESERVE SYSTEM

Assets	Liabilities
"Investments," B_1	Reserve accounts, R

PRIVATE BANKS

Assets	Liabilities
Reserves, R	Deposits, D
Loans, L	
"Investments," B_2	

"Investments" consist of bonds; in practice these are mainly government bonds. The term is put into quotation marks because it is used in the special sense that appears in banking terminology. In terms of the terminology of this book (see Chapter 2), the investments (*not* in quotation marks) made by the Federal Reserve System would be ΔB_1; those made by private banks would be $\Delta(L + B_2)$. This chapter will refer to ΔB_1 as "open market operations," because that is what the Federal Reserve System calls them. The System buys and sells bonds through private brokers and does not deal

[6] Federal Reserve Notes (paper money) are on the liabilities side of the balance sheet. We disregard them for the present.

directly with the Treasury, except in unusual circumstances. When it buys, it pays by check, and these checks are deposited in banks' reserve accounts. When the System sells, it is paid by checks which are then charged to banks' reserve accounts. Such transactions may not occur at all for considerable periods, but if the System wants to intervene in the bond market, it may buy or sell several hundred million dollars of bonds in one week's time. These two balance sheets, expressed symbolically, state that

$$0 = B_1 - R$$

$$0 = R + L + B_2 - D$$

In addition, suppose the total earning assets of the banking system (that is, debt of the nonbanking system) consist either of loans by banks (L) or bonds (B), and that

$$B = B_1 + B_2$$

(all bonds are held by the Federal Reserve System or the private banks). The sale of bonds by borrowing firms or the government, in any period, is ΔB.

Let the banks' demand for reserves be the same as in the Tiny Model:

$$R = rD + F_R$$

where F_R, as before, is *excess reserves*; rD is *required reserves*; and r the *reserve ratio*.

Finally, suppose that Federal Reserve can vary its "investments" at will. Then

$$F_F = B_1$$

Therefore, the variable-into-factor mapping of this theory is written:

$$(\mathbf{F_F, 0, B, F_R, 0}) = (\mathbf{B_1, B_2, R, L, D}) \begin{pmatrix} 1 & 1 & 1 & 0 & 0 \\ 0 & 0 & 1 & 0 & 1 \\ 0 & -1 & 0 & 1 & 1 \\ 0 & 0 & 0 & 0 & 1 \\ 0 & 0 & 0 & -r & -1 \end{pmatrix}$$

The inverse form of this theory is

$$(\mathbf{F_F, 0, B, F_R, 0}) \begin{pmatrix} 1 & -1 & 1 & \frac{1}{r} & \frac{1}{r} \\ 0 & 0 & -1 & \frac{r-1}{r} & -\frac{1}{r} \\ 0 & 1 & 0 & -1 & 0 \\ 0 & 0 & 0 & -\frac{1}{r} & -\frac{1}{r} \\ 0 & 0 & 0 & 1 & 0 \end{pmatrix} = (\mathbf{B_1, B_2, R, L, D})$$

Table 5.1 interprets this simple monetary system. When the Federal Reserve System buys bonds, it reduces bank "investments" by the same amount

Table 5.1. The Implications of Theory 4

THE EFFECT OF A UNIT CHANGE ON	*The Effect of a Unit Change in*		
	F_F (OPEN MARKET OPERATIONS)	B (NEW BOND ISSUES)	F_R (EXCESS RESERVES)
B_2 (Bank holdings of bonds)	-1	1	0
R (Bank reserves)	1	0	0
L (Bank loans)	$\frac{1}{r}$	-1	$-\frac{1}{r}$
D (Bank deposits)	$\frac{1}{r}$	0	$-\frac{1}{r}$

because all bonds are assumed to be held by Federal Reserve and banks. These purchases increase bank reserves by an equal amount; and the banks increase their loans and deposits by $1/r$. This quantity is greater than 1, because r, the reserve ratio, is less than 1. (Remember that deposits are the only kind of money.)

The money supply (D) is unaffected by the sale of new bonds. When new bonds are sold, the banks buy them and reduce their direct loans to customers by an equal amount. This particular feature of the theory is of some interest in terms of government policy. If the bonds are issued because of a government deficit, the sale of bonds automatically reduces bank loans to business (and/or mortgage loans to households), and does *not* lead to an expansion of the money supply. Indeed, if investment is financed from bank loans, government deficits bring about automatic declines in investment by business. For example, in 1966, when government spending on the Viet Nam war rose sharply, the Federal Reserve System was anxious to prevent increases in the money supply. The increased government borrowing led to considerable shortages of credit for business and a major drop in housing construction. With only moderate oversimplification, the decline in housing construction in 1966 can be explained in this fashion.

A change in the banks' desire to have more reserves than Federal Reserve requirements does not affect total reserves. Taken alone, it does not affect the bond holdings of banks. It does, of course, affect loans and the amount of deposits.

Problem Suppose a government has a deficit of X dollars, and that the Federal Reserve System decides that this deficit should not be allowed to change the amount of bank lending. What will it do?

Of course, this discussion deals with the banking system without any reference to the nonbanking sector. Consequently, it can deal with the nonbanking system only indirectly, as the discussion of the 1966 situation indicates. It is natural to see what happens to the rest of the economy.

THEORY 5: BANKING AND THE INTEREST RATE

Nothing has been heard about the interest rate since Theory 1, although some fairly plausible reasons were given for treating it as something which affected investment and hence the whole economy. By making one small change in Theory 5, we can make it into a theory involving the rate of interest. However, let us first consider the strategy to be pursued.

Banks have two kinds of earning assets. They make loans directly to individual customers and they buy bonds (mostly United States Government, state, and local government bonds) on the open market. The interest rates that banks charge their customers are clearly stated on the IOU signed by the customer. The rate of interest earned by banks (or anyone else, for that matter) on bonds purchased in the market requires more explanation.

Government and business bonds are traded every day in the bond market. Also, their prices vary from day to day. These price changes do not affect at all the books of the issuer because his obligations are written, once and for all, on the bond itself.

Why should the price of bonds vary? The answer, obviously, is that some days people will pay more for a given bond issue than other days. The reason is that some days they have more alternative uses for their free cash than on other days.

Let us return to Tiny Model 3, concerning prices. This theory supposed that the quantity of any goods that people were willing to buy depended on the price of those goods. For bonds, in particular,

$$B = ep + F_D$$

The theory also said that the quantity of any goods people were willing to sell depended on the price of those goods. For bonds, in particular,

$$B = fp + F_S$$

But this "supply" of bonds relates to the total amount of this kind of debt which businesses and government wish to have. Suppose that we take the bonds in the market as given (on any particular day they may be). Then the supply equation is replaced by the fixed number:

$$B = \bar{B}$$

Bond prices, then, are given by substitution:

$$\bar{B} = ep + F_D$$

$$p = \frac{\bar{B} - F_D}{e}$$

Changes in bond prices will follow the rule

$$\Delta p = \frac{\Delta\bar{B} - \Delta F_D}{e}$$

Since the higher bond prices are, the fewer bonds people will presumably wish to hold, $e < 0$. Consequently, if $\bar{B}$ increases, p will decrease, and if F_D increases, p will increase.

When the price of bonds changes, the interest rate also changes. This statement at first seems surprising, but it is clear enough on reflection. Suppose a bond has a face value V, it matures in t years, and its holder (whoever he may happen to be at the time) receives C dollars in income for each year it was outstanding. Then a purchaser supposes, when he buys the bond, that he will receive a total of $V + Ct$ if he holds it until maturity. Suppose he pays a price of P dollars for the bond. Then the return on his investment will be given by the formula[7]

$$P(1 + i)^t = V + Ct$$

Here i is the interest rate, and $(1 + i)^t$ is the ordinary compound interest formula, measuring the rate of return on a one-dollar investment held t years. Thus, if the market price P is known, one may evaluate i:

$$(1 + i)^t = \frac{V + Ct}{P}$$

$$i = \left(\frac{V + Ct}{P}\right)^{1/t} - 1$$

If the market rate of interest is known, one may evaluate the price:

$$P = \frac{V + Ct}{(1 + i)^t}$$

In other words, the higher the rate of interest, the smaller the price which an investor will pay for his bond. Alternatively, the higher the market price of bonds, the smaller the return an investor gets from buying them

Thus the interest rate and the price of bonds move in opposite directions, for purely arithmetical reasons. Now let us return to Theory 5. This theory

[7] This approximation says that the coupon return is not invested. If it is reinvested, a more exact formula is

$$P(1 + i)^t = V + \frac{c}{t}[(1 + i)^t - 1]$$

said that bonds were issued by nonbank businesses, and that the total bonds issued (B) were equal to the bond holdings of Federal Reserve (B_1) and the banks (B_2). But the statement $B = B_1 + B_2$ means that the evaluation of the bond issues by nonbanks is the same as that of the bondholders. In other words, the price of bonds is fixed, because if the price of bonds varies, bondholders may pay more or less for their bonds than the amount that the bonds are carried at in the books of the issuers.

Let us drop this statement, and find another that will work as Tiny Model 3 tells us the bond market should work. If bank demand for bonds is

$$B_2 = eR + F_B$$

just as in the Tiny Model, and if the other four statements of Theory 4 are retained, then

$$(\mathbf{F_F, 0, F_B, F_R, 0}) = (\mathbf{B_1, B_2, R, L, D})\begin{pmatrix} 1 & 1 & 0 & 0 & 0 \\ 0 & 0 & 1 & 0 & 1 \\ 0 & -1 & -e & 1 & 1 \\ 0 & 0 & 0 & 0 & 1 \\ 0 & 0 & 0 & -r & -1 \end{pmatrix}$$

The only difference between this matrix and that of Theory 5 is that $-e$ now appears in row 3, column 3. The inverse mapping is

$$(\mathbf{F_F, 0, F_B, F_R, 0})\begin{pmatrix} 1 & e & 1 & -\left(e + \dfrac{r-1}{r}\right) & \dfrac{1}{r} \\ 0 & -e & -1 & \left(e + \dfrac{r-1}{r}\right) & -\dfrac{1}{r} \\ 0 & 1 & 0 & -1 & 0 \\ 0 & 0 & 0 & -\dfrac{1}{r} & -\dfrac{1}{r} \\ 0 & 0 & 0 & 1 & 0 \end{pmatrix} = (\mathbf{B_1, B_2, R, L, D})$$

We may now consider the implications of Theory 5, as shown in Table 5.2.

The change in the valuation of bonds held by bondholders is the sum $(\Delta B_1 + \Delta B_2)$. There is no change in the number of bonds issued by nonbanks. Consequently, if $(\Delta B_1 + \Delta B_2)$ is *positive*, the price of bonds *rises*, and the interest rate *falls*.

Theory 5 implies that change in excess reserves does not affect the interest rate, because banks change only their loans and not their investments in bonds to acquire excess reserves. This result is the consequence of the simple form of Theory 4. Most economists would expect loans and bondholdings to move in the same direction in this case.

An increase in bank demand for bonds in this theory causes banks to

Table 5.2. The Implications of Theory 5

	The Effect of		
THE EFFECT UPON	OPEN MARKET OPERATIONS (ΔF_F)	INCREASED BANK DEMAND FOR BONDS (ΔF_B)	INCREASED EXCESS RESERVES (ΔF_B)
Federal reserve Bondholdings (ΔB_1)	1	0	0
Private bank bondholdings (ΔB_2)	e	1	0
Bank reserves (ΔR)	1	0	0
Bank loans (ΔL)	$-\left(e + \frac{r-1}{r}\right)$	-1	$-\frac{1}{r}$
Bank deposits (ΔD)	$\frac{1}{r}$	0	$-\frac{1}{r}$

reduce loans by the same amount that bondholdings rise. In this case, the yield on bonds would fall.

It is plausible to expect the interest rate on loans and on bonds to move in generally the same direction. Banks, after all, have a choice between the two kinds of assets. But bonds are more easily converted into cash than are loans; so this last result is not impossible under suitable conditions.

Finally, if the Federal Reserve System buys \$1.00 of bonds, the private banks are led to buy \$$e$ of bonds. Since $e < 0$, private bank bond holdings *decline* by \$$e$. The sign of $(1 + e)$ is not clear, since it is not known whether $e \geq -1$ or $e < -1$. Thus we can be sure that the money supply rises ($\Delta D = 1/r > 0$), but we cannot be sure what happens to the interest rate, or to the level of bank loans.

This analysis is a short, incomplete description of the relation between the banking system and the interest rate. It is not possible to compute the actual level or the change in the interest rate. The formula used,

$$i = \left(\frac{V + Ct}{P}\right)^{1/t} - 1$$

is only an approximation. Moreover, there is no way of determining in our theory either the annual coupon (C) or the maturity date (t) of bonds. For this reason, only the *direction* of change of the interest rate can now be given.

Actually, the theory just outlined is unsatisfactory in that it takes the number of bonds outstanding as given. In order to be a complete account of the economy, a theory would have to answer what determines the number of bonds outstanding. Such a theory would take into account nonbank balance sheets as well as bank balance sheets.

But it is helpful to have a theory that tells something about the interest rate, although the interest rate does not appear as an explicit variable of the theory. The interest rate appears in a different way here from some points of view, this way of handling the interest rate is a much neater way than that used in Theory 1, where the interest rate appears as an explicit variable.

MONETARY THEORIES AND INCOME THEORIES

This chapter has presented a Tiny Model and Theories 4 and 5. The variables whose values are determined by the three are as follows:

Tiny Model 4 determined:	Money
	Bank loans
Theories 4 and 5 determined:	Bank holdings of bonds
	Bank reserves
	Bank loans
	Bank deposits

Theory 5 also implicitly determined the interest rate. No explicit calculation of the interest rate was given, for the formula would be complicated.

These variables are quite different from the variables determined in Theories 1 to 3: consumption, investment, the interest rate, tax revenue the national product. At first guess, we might be tempted to say that the theories in this chapter really have nothing to do with those in Chapter 4, because, after all, they are concerned with quite different variables.

However, let us recall what has been said about investment. In Tiny Model 2, we said that suppose the amount of plant which businesses want to have depends on their total assets. If something is done to change the money supply, total assets will change, and therefore the volume of plant desired by business will change. Investment is the change in plant; therefore, a change in the money supply creates a demand for investment.

In Theory 1, we reasoned that the demand for investment depends partly on the interest rate. The demand for consumer goods depends partly on the money supply. If there is a change in the banking sector, so that the interest rate and bank deposits both change, then these changes will have an effect on the variables of Theory 1.

Theories 2 and 3 would seem to have no such direct connection with the banking theories. But if the government has a deficit, then *either* it must borrow the sum needed to pay for its purchases, *or* it must print paper money. Once credit and money enter the discussion, a connection has been made to the theories in this chapter.

The conclusions drawn from monetary theories, therefore, are related to the subjects in the income theories. At this point, however, readers may be able to see a relation, but may not be able to specify just how the connection might work out. It is the function of the next chapter to fit the two ways of thought into a single system.

6

MONEY AND THE NATIONAL INCOME

This chapter combines theories about national product, nonbank balance sheets, and bank balance sheets into a unified system. Thus it brings together the main ideas in Chapters 4 and 5. It also sets forth the central issue in macroeconomics: do households and businesses decide on their purchases by looking at their current income or by looking at their assets? The working of the economy depend on which form of behavior is actually followed.

To show the importance of these alternative behavioral patterns, four versions of the theory are set forth. These lead to quite different conclusions:

Theory 6A says: The Federal Reserve System influences the commercial banks, consumers, and businesses. Businesses influence consumers but not banks. Consumers influence nobody.

Theory 6B says: The Federal Reserve System and the commercial banks both influence consumers and businesses. Consumers and businesses influence nobody.

Theory 6C says: The banking system influences nobody. Consumers and businesses influence each other but not the banking system.

Theory 6D says: Consumers, businesses, and the Federal Reserve System all influence the commercial banks. The commercial banks influence nobody.

Readers cannot select one "correct theory" from this set, any more than can professional economists. But the reader should be able to understand how important it is for economists to find out how, in fact, economic units do make their decisions.

AN EXPURGATED HISTORY OF THE SUBJECT

Historically, the connection between income and money went through a number of stages. It is helpful to summarize these stages, for they contain useful ideas. The first stage is associated with the so-called *monetary identity:*

$$MV = PQ$$

Imagine that the money supply consists of dollar bills, and that whenever they change hands, the person making the payment signs his name on the bill. Every time there is a business transaction, some quantity of goods is sold at a certain price, and also dollar bills are signed by the buyers of goods. At the end of the day (or week or month), we determine the average number of signatures on the dollar bills. This number measures the "velocity" (V) with which money changes hands; the product of V and the number of dollars M, therefore, is a precise measure of the value of the goods which changed hands.

Also, $1/V$ measures the average length of time that people hold a dollar bill. The greater $1/V$ is, the longer people hold onto their money before spending it. Of course, the greater $1/V$ is, the less velocity is. We may therefore associate, very roughly, $1/V$ with the tendency of people to hold their cash, rather than to spend it. Thus $1/V$ may be associated with what has been called *savings* in connection with income accounting. Obviously the association is indirect, but it is real.

In Tiny Model 1, it was shown that

$$Y = \frac{1}{1 - a}(I + F_C)$$

If money were used only for income transactions (so that there were no purchases or sales of any assets), velocity would be

$$V = \frac{Y}{M} = \frac{(I + F_C)}{(1 - a)M}$$

In this case, increases in investment (I), in autonomous consumption (F_C), or in the marginal propensity to consume $(1 - a)$ would all increase velocity, given any amount of money. Since holding money is (in this theory) an alternative to spending (whether on investment or consumption), increases in a "generalized willingness to spend" can be associated with increases in velocity (V), and with decreases in the average time ($1/V$) a dollar is held.

In Theory 1, it was shown that

$$Y = \frac{1}{1 - a}\left(F_C + F_I - \frac{b + d}{e}F_L + \frac{b + ev + d}{e}M\right)$$

so that (again assuming no asset transactions)

$$V = \frac{Y}{M} = \frac{b + ev + d}{e(1 - a)} + \frac{\left(F_C + F_I - \dfrac{b + d}{e} F_L\right)}{(1 - a)M}$$

This case is consistent with Tiny Model 1, but we now see directly that an increase in the demand for money ($\Delta F_L > 0$) means a decrease in velocity, because $(b + d)/e > 0$. Consequently, $1/v$ decreases as F_L increases.

These two theories are both more precise and more simple than the literature on velocity. They are more precise in the sense that they are based on explicit national income theories, which did not exist in the 1920s. These theories show that for any vector of factors, a numerical value for V may be calculated. They are simpler in two respects. First, all the relations involved are linear. Second, they ignore the existence of transactions involving assets. Even if the total assets of the community were constant, we should expect that there would be transfers of these assets among businesses and individuals. Thus the formulas given here relate only to "income velocity."

The formulas used here take velocity as something to be explained. The earlier literature tended to regard velocity as a given number. That is, V was taken as a given number, just as, in the relation between consumption and the amount of money of Theory 1,

$$C = aY + vL + bR + F_C$$

v was taken to be a given number. If velocity is a given number V, then we may theorize about the effects of changes in the money supply (M) on the rest of the monetary identity $MV = PQ$.

The business transactions involved many kinds of goods and hence many different prices. But P may be taken as an "average price," or measure of the price level, and Q as an "average quantity," or a measure of the quantity of goods produced. (There are important practical problems in measuring P and Q, but let us suppose these solved.)

Suppose the quantity of money (M) is changed, but that V (the willingness, roughly speaking, of people to hold money) is fixed. Then, of course, either the price level (P) or output (Q) must change. If the economy is operating at capacity so that there is no unemployment, output cannot increase as money increases. Thus, with fixed $V = \bar{V}$ and $Q = \bar{Q}$,

$$M\bar{V} = \bar{Q}P$$

$$M = \left(\frac{\bar{Q}}{\bar{V}}\right)P$$

and prices will vary in proportion to the quantity of money.

If there is idle capacity and unemployment, then (it was said), prices may be taken as given ($P = \bar{P}$); if V is constant, then

$$M\bar{V} = \bar{P}Q$$

$$M = \left(\frac{\bar{P}}{\bar{V}}\right) Q$$

so that output varies with the money supply.

This form of the relation between money and income was seen to be unsatisfactory when the first measures of the national income were developed. For not all business transactions relate to income. Some payments of money are associated with transfers of assets. To surmount this difficulty, it was assumed (in effect) that transfers of assets were proportional to income transactions, and therefore,

$$MV = Y$$

Here V must be redefined as "income velocity" and Y, of course, is the national product. In this form, the "quantity theory" asserts a relation between national income and the quantity of money. If velocity is constant, then the two vary proportionately. If V is related to national income in some suitable way, then it is still possible to express income in terms of the quantity of money. Assume, for instance, that for some reason,

$$V = aY + b$$

Then

$$M(aY + b) = Y$$

$$b = Y(1 - aM)$$

$$Y = \frac{b}{1 - aM}$$

If M increases, it may be shown that Y will increase providing a and b are both positive or both negative, and both fixed. The second case may be ruled out since both M and Y are inherently positive.

Actually, it has turned out to be relatively simple to disentangle these matters, once the idea of including the social accounts as a systematic part of a theory became accepted. There are three relevant pieces to the economy: the income accounts, the balance sheets of nonbanks, and the balance sheets of banks. Money certainly appears as a component of the last two sets of accounts, and the assertion to be studied is that the banks may affect national income.

In earlier chapters, we have shown that there may be simple or complicated theories pertaining to each of the sets of accounts. It is natural, however, to return to the simplest theory possible in considering any new problem. Therefore, the connection between money and the national income will be considered in its very simplest form. This approach is justified because a new "operation" is being undertaken: the combination of related theories.

COMBINING THE INCOME AND MONETARY ACCOUNTS

Most studies of macroeconomics start with some very simple notion, which may then be elaborated into a more complicated structure. Three very simple starting points have been presented. Tiny Model 1, dealing with the national income; Tiny Model 2, dealing with (nonbank) balance sheets; and Tiny Model 4, dealing with bank balance sheets. These three Tiny Models all have the same structure. That is, with each model there is associated a matrix having the form

$$\begin{pmatrix} 1 & -x \\ -1 & 1 \end{pmatrix}$$

The symbol designated x here is in each case a number between 0 and 1; each number has a different economic interpretation in each of the Tiny Models. In Tiny Model 1, x was replaced by a, the "marginal propensity to consume," which designates the proportion of a dollar's increase in income which is consumed. In Tiny Model 2, x was replaced by b, which designates the proportion of a dollar's increase in assets which is used to buy more plant. In Tiny Model 4, x was replaced by $(1 - r)$, where r is the "reserve requirement," designating the proportion of a dollar's increase in deposits which the banks must hold in the form of cash (reserves).

In each of the chapters so far, a Tiny Model has been imbedded in some larger system. Additional factors and variables have been taken into the theory, so as to make it closer to ordinary experience and to be able to account for larger classes of observable events.

But each chapter has tended to be isolated from the others. There is some overlap in subject matter, as is shown by the overlap in the list of factors and variables. This overlap, however, is not really a combination of theories into a uniform way of looking at the economy. This combination may be effected at various levels of complexity. For example, the theories about the national income were of various degrees of difficulty. Tiny Model 1 was the simplest version; Theory 1 involved the interest rate, but not government; Theories 2 and 3 involved government, but not the interest rate. It would have been possible to present a theory involving the interest rate and also government. To combine theories about income with theories about bank and nonbank balance sheets, some level of complexity must be specified.

At the end of Chapter 3, block notation was described. This notation is a compact way of writing down theories which otherwise might have large and complicated matrices. The use of block notation will considerably simplify the present discussion, for it is possible to represent the Tiny Models as blocks that are to be combined to form a theory about an entire economy.

The three Tiny Models may be written down separately as

$$\mathbf{F}_1 = \mathbf{V}_1\mathbf{M}_1 \quad \text{in the case of Tiny Model 1}$$
$$\mathbf{F}_2 = \mathbf{V}_2\mathbf{M}_2 \quad \text{in the case of Tiny Model 2}$$
$$\mathbf{F}_4 = \mathbf{V}_4\mathbf{M}_4 \quad \text{in the case of Tiny Model 4}$$

Each M_i stands for a matrix of the form $\begin{pmatrix} 1 & -x \\ -1 & 1 \end{pmatrix}$. Each F_i and V_i stands for a vector with two components. If the three Tiny Models were really independent of each other, we could write a single theory to encompass them all:

$$(\mathbf{F}_1, \mathbf{F}_2, \mathbf{F}_4) = (\mathbf{V}_1, \mathbf{V}_2, \mathbf{V}_4) \begin{pmatrix} M_1 & 0 & 0 \\ 0 & M_2 & 0 \\ 0 & 0 & M_4 \end{pmatrix} = (\mathbf{V}_1\mathbf{M}_1, \mathbf{V}_2\mathbf{M}_2, \mathbf{V}_3\mathbf{M}_3)$$

For each block F_i on the left, there would be a block V_iM_i on the right. These would each represent, respectively, one of the Tiny Models.

(1) If this procedure were adopted, then when block notation was replaced by ordinary vector notation,

$$(\mathbf{F}_1, \mathbf{F}_2, \mathbf{F}_3) = (\mathbf{I}, \mathbf{F_C}, \mathbf{M}, \mathbf{F_K}, \mathbf{R}, \mathbf{F_L})$$

$$(\mathbf{V}_1, \mathbf{V}_2, \mathbf{V}_4) = (\mathbf{Y}, \mathbf{C}, \mathbf{W}, \mathbf{K}, \mathbf{M}, \mathbf{L})$$

An obvious difficulty is that M, the amount of money, appears both as a factor and as a variable. There is no reason why there should not be some theories (such as Tiny Model 2) in which M is a factor, and others (such as Tiny Model 4), in which M is a variable, provided these theories are recognized as distinct. But when theories are put together, the "product" must exhibit a systematic and consistent treatment of the parts. Therefore, M cannot be on both sides of the equation.

It is possible to take care of this difficulty by treating M solely as a variable. This means rewriting the system:

$$(\mathbf{I}, \mathbf{F_C}, \mathbf{0}, \mathbf{F_K}, \mathbf{R}, \mathbf{F_L}) = (\mathbf{Y}, \mathbf{C}, \mathbf{W}, \mathbf{K}, \mathbf{M}, \mathbf{L}) \begin{pmatrix} 1 & -a & 0 & 0 & 0 & 0 \\ -1 & 1 & 0 & 0 & 0 & 0 \\ 0 & 0 & 1 & -b & 0 & 0 \\ 0 & 0 & -1 & 1 & 0 & 0 \\ 0 & 0 & -1 & 0 & 1 & -s \\ 0 & 0 & 0 & 0 & -1 & 1 \end{pmatrix}$$

[*Note:* In this chapter, we will use the notation $s = 1 - r$, where r is the reserve requirement.]

(2) Now an inconsistency appears in the balance sheet sector of the economy. The banks make loans, which appear as part of their assets. These loans presumably represent debts of the nonbanks, but as now defined, the nonbanks do not have any debts. When this inconsistency is removed,

$$(\mathbf{I}, \mathbf{F_C}, \mathbf{0}, \mathbf{F_K}, \mathbf{R}, \mathbf{F_L}) = (\mathbf{Y}, \mathbf{C}, \mathbf{W}, \mathbf{K}, \mathbf{M}, \mathbf{L}) \begin{pmatrix} 1 & -a & 0 & 0 & 0 & 0 \\ -1 & 1 & 0 & 0 & 0 & 0 \\ 0 & 0 & 1 & -b & 0 & 0 \\ 0 & 0 & -1 & 1 & 0 & 0 \\ 0 & 0 & -1 & 0 & 1 & -s \\ 0 & 0 & 1 & 0 & -1 & 1 \end{pmatrix}$$

In block form, this theory is

$$(\mathbf{F_1}, \mathbf{F_2}, \mathbf{F_4}) = (\mathbf{V_1}, \mathbf{V_2}, \mathbf{V_4}) \begin{pmatrix} M_1 & 0 & 0 \\ 0 & M_2 & 0 \\ 0 & M_{42} & M_4 \end{pmatrix}$$

The inverse form of this system is

$$(\mathbf{Y}, \mathbf{C}, \mathbf{W}, \mathbf{K}, \mathbf{M}, \mathbf{L}) = (\mathbf{I}, \mathbf{F_C}, \mathbf{0}, \mathbf{F_K}, \mathbf{R}, \mathbf{F_L}) \begin{pmatrix} \frac{1}{1-a} & \frac{a}{1-a} & 0 & 0 & 0 & 0 \\ \frac{1}{1-a} & \frac{1}{1-a} & 0 & 0 & 0 & 0 \\ 0 & 0 & \frac{1}{1-b} & \frac{b}{1-b} & 0 & 0 \\ 0 & 0 & \frac{1}{1-b} & \frac{1}{1-b} & 0 & 0 \\ 0 & 0 & \frac{1}{1-b} & \frac{b}{1-b} & \frac{1}{1-s} & \frac{s}{1-s} \\ 0 & 0 & 0 & 0 & \frac{1}{1-s} & \frac{1}{1-s} \end{pmatrix}$$

The interpretation of this inverse form is given in Table 6.1. For convenience, we label this theory as Theory 6.

Theory 6 seems to have some curious implications, as Table 6.1 indicates.

(1) If investment rises, plant remains fixed. But in Chapter 2 it was shown that investment is the change in plant; an increase in investment must increase the amount of plant.

(2) Investment is presumably financed either from savings (an increase in net worth), by a reduction in cash balances, or by an increase in debt. But

Table 6.1. The Implications of Theory 6

THE EFFECT OF A UNIT INCREASE OF	*The Effect upon* NATIONAL PRODUCT	CONSUMPTION	NET WORTH	PLANT	MONEY	BANK LOANS
Investment (ΔI)	$\frac{1}{1-a}$	$\frac{a}{1-a}$	0	0	0	0
Consumer demand (ΔF_C)	$\frac{1}{1-a}$	$\frac{1}{1-a}$	0	0	0	0
Demand for plant (ΔF_K)	0	0	$\frac{1}{1-b}$	$\frac{1}{1-b}$	0	0
Bank reserves (ΔR)	0	0	$\frac{1}{1-b}$	$\frac{b}{1-b}$	$\frac{1}{1-s}$	$\frac{s}{1-s}$
Supply of bank loans (ΔF_L)	0	0	0	0	$\frac{1}{1-s}$	$\frac{1}{1-s}$

[*Note:* From Chapter 5, remember that if the demand for reserves is $R = rM + F_R$, the supply of loans is $L = (1 - r)M + F_L$, where $F_L = -F_R$.]

Table 6.1 states that it is possible to increase investment with no change in *any* of these variables.

(3) If the amount of plant increases (as was shown in Chapter 2), there is investment, and investment is a part of the national product. But in Table 6.1, the factor changes, which affect the national product, do not affect the total level of plant; and the factor changes, which affect the level of plant, do not affect the national product.

In one way or another, these various difficulties all involve investment. So far, there is nothing that explicitly links investment to the balance sheet system of Tiny Model 2. If we introduce the definition $K = K_0 + I$, which says that plant in the given period (K) is equal to plant in the previous period (K_0) plus new plant ($\Delta K \equiv I$), and if we make an investment, like plant (a variable), then system 6A is obtained:

$$(\mathbf{0}, \mathbf{F_C}, \mathbf{K_0}, \mathbf{0}, \mathbf{F_K}, \mathbf{R}, \mathbf{F_L}) = (\mathbf{Y}, \mathbf{C}, \mathbf{I}, \mathbf{W}, \mathbf{K}, \mathbf{M}, \mathbf{L}) \begin{pmatrix} 1 & -a & 0 & 0 & 0 & 0 & 0 \\ -1 & 1 & 0 & 0 & 0 & 0 & 0 \\ -1 & 0 & -1 & 0 & 0 & 0 & 0 \\ 0 & 0 & 0 & 1 & -b & 0 & 0 \\ 0 & 0 & 1 & -1 & 1 & 0 & 0 \\ 0 & 0 & 0 & -1 & 0 & 1 & -s \\ 0 & 0 & 0 & 1 & 0 & -1 & 1 \end{pmatrix}$$

The number of variables and factors has been increased from six to seven. In block form, Theory 6A is not quite like Theory 6:

$$(\hat{\mathbf{F}}_1, \hat{\mathbf{F}}_2, \hat{\mathbf{F}}_4) = (\hat{\mathbf{V}}_1, \hat{\mathbf{V}}_2, \hat{\mathbf{V}}_4) \begin{pmatrix} M_1 & 0 & 0 \\ M_{21} & M_2 & 0 \\ 0 & M_{42} & M_4 \end{pmatrix}$$

This is because the block M_{21} is zero in 6 and not zero in 6A. Moreover, M_2 has become a 3×3 matrix, so that the second row and the second column of blocks is different in 6A than in 6.

Has any improvement in performance been brought about? The inverse form of Theory 6A is

$$(\mathbf{Y}, \mathbf{C}, \mathbf{I}, \mathbf{W}, \mathbf{K}, \mathbf{M}, \mathbf{L}) = (\mathbf{0}, \mathbf{F_C}, \mathbf{K_0}, \mathbf{0}, \mathbf{F_K}, \mathbf{R}, \mathbf{F_L})$$

$$\begin{pmatrix} \frac{1}{1-a} & \frac{a}{1-a} & 0 & 0 & 0 & 0 & 0 \\ \frac{1}{1-a} & \frac{1}{1-a} & 0 & 0 & 0 & 0 & 0 \\ \frac{-1}{1-a} & \frac{-a}{1-a} & -1 & 0 & 0 & 0 & 0 \\ \frac{b}{(1-a)(1-b)} & \frac{ab}{(1-a)(1-b)} & \frac{b}{1-b} & \frac{1}{1-b} & \frac{b}{1-b} & 0 & 0 \\ \frac{1}{(1-a)(1-b)} & \frac{a}{(1-a)(1-b)} & \frac{1}{1-b} & \frac{1}{1-b} & \frac{1}{1-b} & 0 & 0 \\ \frac{b}{(1-a)(1-b)} & \frac{ab}{(1-a)(1-b)} & \frac{b}{1-b} & \frac{1}{1-b} & \frac{b}{1-b} & \frac{1}{1-s} & \frac{s}{1-s} \\ 0 & 0 & 0 & 0 & 0 & \frac{1}{1-s} & \frac{1}{1-s} \end{pmatrix}$$

From this inverse form, we deduce the implications given in Table 6.2. This table shows that the particular troubles found in Table 6.1 have indeed been cleared up. Changes in investment are associated with equal changes in plant. Changes in investment are always associated with changes in national product.

Consider the question of financing investment. If F_K (the level of demand for plant) rises by 1, actual plant and investment increase by $1/(1-b)$, and net worth increases by an equal amount. In Chapter 2, savings was shown to be the same as the change in net worth, so in this case savings equals investment. The banking system is unaffected.

On the other hand, when the supply of loans increases by 1, loans increase by $s/(1-s) = 1 - r$ (where r is the reserve requirement). The quantity of money (bank deposits) rises by $1/(1-s)$. The increase in cash assets causes nonbanks to want more plant, in the amount of $b/(1-b)$. Total assets thus

Table 6.2. The Implications of Theory 6A

THE EFFECT OF A UNIT INCREASE IN	The Effect upon						
	NATIONAL PRODUCT	CONSUMPTION	INVEST-MENT	NET WORTH	PLANT	MONEY	BANK LOANS
Consumer demand (ΔF_C)	$\frac{1}{1-a}$	$\frac{1}{1-a}$	0	0	0	0	0
Demand for plant (ΔF_K)	$\frac{1}{(1-a)(1-b)}$	$\frac{a}{(1-a)(1-b)}$	$\frac{1}{1-b}$	$\frac{1}{1-b}$	$\frac{1}{1-b}$	0	0
Bank reserves (ΔR)	$\frac{b}{(1-a)(1-b)}$	$\frac{ab}{(1-a)(1-b)}$	$\frac{b}{1-b}$	$\frac{1}{1-b}$	$\frac{b}{1-b}$	$\frac{1}{1-s}$	$\frac{s}{1-s}$
Supply of loans (ΔF_L)	0	0	0	0	0	$\frac{1}{1-s}$	$\frac{1}{1-s}$

rise by $(1 - bs)/(1 - s)(1 - b)$; this increase is financed from loans in the amount of $s/(1 - s)$ and from savings (net worth) in the amount of $1/(1 - b)$.

An interesting feature of Theory 6A is the following: The Federal Reserve System could affect the national product, but the private banks could not. Changes in bank reserves (which are carried out by the Federal Reserve System) affect all parts of the social accounts. But changes in the supply of loans have only the effect of changing loans and the amount of money by equal amounts. In other words, the private banks would be "neutral," insofar as the level of current output and income are concerned.

This feature of Theory 6A will be unsatisfactory to most monetary theorists. They may argue, in part, that by omitting bond financing, the theory has omitted one of the important features of investment finance. Theory 5 certainly made the private banks influence the level of plant, and hence the amount of investment—a component of output.

But it is not necessary to make Theory 6A more complicated to meet this criticism. It is merely necessary to alter the behavioral assumptions of the theory, and to start off, so to speak, with a different collection of Tiny Models. It might have been difficult to devise Theory 6A starting from the beginning. Given the structure of the theory, however, it is relatively easy to alter it in such a way as to see how the economy would behave if people and businesses acted in somewhat different ways from those specified so far.

ALTERNATIVE PATTERNS OF NONBANK BEHAVIOR

Tiny Model 1 contains a statement about consumer behavior: Consumers look at their incomes and then decide how much to spend. An alternative, but equally simple theory would be the following: Consumers look at the balance in their bank accounts and decide how much to spend. This alternative behavior would be given by the equation

$$C = vM + F_C$$

or equivalently,

$$F_C = C - vM$$

This statement is not unrelated to that in Tiny Model 1. Suppose Mr. Consumer is paid on each Friday, say an amount of \$98.00. If Mrs. Consumer spends exactly \$14.00 per day, she will then have exactly nothing in her bank account when her husband gets home on Friday evening. To put it differently, when half the week is gone, she will have \$49.00 in her bank account; this sum is her average balance over the course of the week. Looking at her spending, we can say either (a) she spends her entire income in the course of the week ($C = Y$), or (b) during the week she spends twice her average bank balance ($V = 2$, $F_C = 0$). Obviously, if she keeps a minimum cash balance, or if she saves a part of her weekly income, different relations will prevail between consumption and income, and also between consumption and bank balances.

Observationally, in any given case one can make either a statement relating consumer spending to income, or a statement relating consumer spending to cash balances. But one can distinguish two quite different ways Mrs. Consumer might decide whether to buy a new dress. (a) She may say, "I will buy the dress, because I have enough money in the bank to pay for it." (That is the decision we are now suggesting.) (b) She may say, "My husband will bring home his check next Friday, and I can therefore afford this dress." (That is the decision suggested by Tiny Model 1.) As we shall see, there is an important distinction between the two kinds of decisions.

Tiny Model 2 contains a statement about business behavior: Businesses look at their total assets and decide how much plant to acquire. Their decision relates to the division of assets between cash and plant. An alternative, but equally simple theory would be the following: Businesses look at their cash balances and decide how much plant they can afford. (If they want more plant, they may either borrow, or use their own funds to pay for it.) This alternative behavior would be given by the equation:

$$K = wM + F_K$$

or equivalently,

$$F_K = K - wM$$

In this case, the business decides whether or not to buy a new factory or a new piece of equipment by looking at its bank account. In this respect, its behavior would be analogous to the behavior of Mrs. Consumer.

Nobody would argue that either the behavior implied by the Tiny Models or the behavior being investigated here matches the complexity of human actions in the real world. However, there is a substantial difference in the workings of the economy whether human behavior is more like that of the Tiny Models or more like that in the present theory. For when these two statements are substituted for the corresponding statements of Theory 6A, a new theory is obtained, which will be called Theory 6B:

$$(\mathbf{0}, \mathbf{F_C}, \mathbf{K_0}, \mathbf{0}, \mathbf{F_K}, \mathbf{R}, \mathbf{F_L}) = (\mathbf{Y}, \mathbf{C}, \mathbf{I}, \mathbf{W}, \mathbf{K}, \mathbf{M}, \mathbf{L}) \begin{pmatrix} 1 & 0 & 0 & 0 & 0 & 0 & 0 \\ -1 & 1 & 0 & 0 & 0 & 0 & 0 \\ -1 & 0 & -1 & 0 & 0 & 0 & 0 \\ 0 & 0 & 0 & 1 & 0 & 0 & 0 \\ 0 & 0 & 1 & -1 & 1 & 0 & 0 \\ 0 & -v & 0 & -1 & -w & 1 & -s \\ 0 & 0 & 0 & 1 & 0 & -1 & 1 \end{pmatrix}$$

The inverse of this equation turns out to be

$$(\mathbf{Y}, \mathbf{C}, \mathbf{I}, \mathbf{W}, \mathbf{K}, \mathbf{M}, \mathbf{L}) = (\mathbf{0}, \mathbf{F_C}, \mathbf{K_0}, \mathbf{0}, \mathbf{F_K}, \mathbf{R}, \mathbf{F_L})$$

$$\begin{pmatrix} 1 & 0 & 0 & 0 & 0 & 0 & 0 \\ 1 & 1 & 0 & 0 & 0 & 0 & 0 \\ -1 & 0 & -1 & 0 & 0 & 0 & 0 \\ 0 & 0 & 0 & 1 & 0 & 0 & 0 \\ 1 & 0 & 1 & 1 & 1 & 0 & 0 \\ \frac{w+v}{1-s} & \frac{v}{1-s} & \frac{w}{1-s} & \frac{1-s+w}{1-s} & \frac{w}{1-s} & \frac{1}{1-s} & \frac{s}{1-s} \\ \frac{w+v}{1-s} & \frac{v}{1-s} & \frac{w}{1-s} & \frac{w}{1-s} & \frac{w}{1-s} & \frac{1}{1-s} & \frac{1}{1-s} \end{pmatrix}$$

Table 6.3. The Implications of Theory 6B

	The Effect upon						
THE EFFECT OF A UNIT INCREASE IN	NATIONAL PRODUCT	CON-SUMP-TION	INVEST-MENT	NET WORTH	PLANT	MONEY	BANK LOANS
Consumer demand (ΔF_C)	1	1	0	0	0	0	0
Demand for plant (ΔF_K)	1	0	1	1	1	0	0
Bank reserves (ΔR)	$\frac{w+v}{1-s}$	$\frac{v}{1-s}$	$\frac{w}{1-s}$	$\frac{1-s+w}{1-s}$	$\frac{w}{1-s}$	$\frac{1}{1-s}$	$\frac{s}{1-s}$
Supply of loans (ΔF_L)	$\frac{w+v}{1-s}$	$\frac{v}{1-s}$	$\frac{w}{1-s}$	$\frac{w}{1-s}$	$\frac{w}{1-s}$	$\frac{1}{1-s}$	$\frac{1}{1-s}$

One obvious difference between the implications of Theory 6B (Table 6.3) and Theory 6A (Table 6.2) is that in 6B the banking system can influence the national product. That is, the elements of the last row of Table 6.3 are nonzero. The first five elements of the last row of Table 6.2 were all zeros.

In this theory, velocity of cash balances of consumers (v) and businesses (w) have replaced the marginal propensity to consume (a) and the plant coefficient (b) of Theory 6A. Consequently, when investment rises, there is no induced effect on consumer spending; and when the demand for plant rises, there is no induced effect upon cash balances demanded. Thus the terms, $(1 - a)$ and $(1 - b)$, appearing in the denominator of terms in Table 6.2 do not appear here. Generally speaking, this system is insensitive to changes in the nonmonetary variables, because it was constructed that way.

HISTORICAL REMARK

Table 6.2 makes it possible to explain why economists have abandoned theories such as Theory 1 (in which money appears as a factor) in favor of theories in which all balance sheets accounts appear as variables.

When World War II began, there was large-scale unemployment in the United States. Between the German occupation of France (June 1940) and Pearl Harbor (December 1941) there was a large increase in government spending. By the spring of 1942 unemployment had disappeared, and the government began to try to persuade housewives to take jobs. As the end of the war approached in 1944–1945, professional economists, who then thought in terms of Theory 2, predicted as follows: Government spending rose from $9 billion in 1939 to $95 billion in 1944, and unemployment disappeared. When the war ends, this spending will certainly drop. If it dropped back to the prewar level, we should expect (by Theory 2) a return to prewar unemployment levels.

Of course, the above did not happen. In particular, consumers spent much more in 1946–1947 than anyone would have predicted. Some people said, "Aha! F_C has increased." But others said that the reason consumers were spending so much more was that they had so much *cash*. Why? Well, during the war, automobiles and other durable goods had not been available, so consumers had saved more than usual, and some of this savings was in cash. Moreover, the Federal Reserve System had bought large amounts of government bonds, so the money supply had greatly increased. If Theory 6B were true, then an increase in bank reserves would increase the national product. Even if government spending should fall, the economy would not return to its prewar condition because Federal Reserve action during the war would make such a return impossible.

This account, as usual, is oversimplified. It is the case, however, that the unification of income and balance sheet theories was greatly speeded by the puzzle that economists found in our unexpected prosperity after World War II. Theory 2 simply turned out to be wrong, and theories such as Theory 6 (although more complicated) have come to replace it.

Many economists have been reluctant to give the banking system as much importance as it has in Theory 6B. For them, money is merely a tool, and they cannot imagine it influencing "real" things like the production of goods. It is natural to show, in the context of Theory 6, a theory with "neutral money," which will be numbered Theory 6C.

In Theory 6C, consumer spending depends on income, as in Tiny Model 1:

$$C = aY + F_C$$

The demand for plant, however, will be different from any of the statements made so far:

$$K = xY + F_K$$

That is, the amount of plant that businesses want will depend partly on the level of output. It is easy to interpret the amount of plant in terms of "industrial capacity," so that the amount of capacity needed by businesses depend on the volume of output (Y) which businesses are called upon to supply to the public.

If these two behavioral statements were true, the theory would be:

$$(\mathbf{0}, \mathbf{F_C}, \mathbf{K_0}, \mathbf{0}, \mathbf{F_K}, \mathbf{R}, \mathbf{F_L}) = (\mathbf{Y}, \mathbf{C}, \mathbf{I}, \mathbf{W}, \mathbf{K}, \mathbf{M}, \mathbf{L}) \begin{pmatrix} 1 & -a & 0 & 0 & -x & 0 & 0 \\ -1 & 1 & 0 & 0 & 0 & 0 & 0 \\ -1 & 0 & -1 & 0 & 0 & 0 & 0 \\ 0 & 0 & 0 & 1 & 0 & 0 & 0 \\ 0 & 0 & 1 & -1 & 1 & 0 & 0 \\ 0 & 0 & 0 & -1 & 0 & 1 & -s \\ 0 & 0 & 0 & 1 & 0 & -1 & 1 \end{pmatrix}$$

The inverse form of this theory is

$$(\mathbf{Y}, \mathbf{C}, \mathbf{I}, \mathbf{W}, \mathbf{K}, \mathbf{M}, \mathbf{L}) = (\mathbf{0}, \mathbf{F_C}, \mathbf{K_0}, \mathbf{0}, \mathbf{F_K}, \mathbf{R}, \mathbf{F_L})$$

$$\begin{pmatrix} \frac{1}{1-x-a} & \frac{a}{1-x-a} & \frac{x}{1-x-a} & \frac{x}{1-x-a} & \frac{x}{1-x-a} & 0 & 0 \\ \frac{1}{1-x-a} & \frac{1-x}{1-x-a} & \frac{x}{1-x-a} & \frac{x}{1-x-a} & \frac{x}{1-x-a} & 0 & 0 \\ \frac{-1}{1-x-a} & \frac{-a}{1-x-a} & \frac{1-a}{1-x-a} & \frac{-x}{1-x-a} & \frac{-x}{1-x-a} & 0 & 0 \\ 0 & 0 & 0 & 0 & 1 & 0 & 0 \\ \frac{1}{1-x-a} & \frac{a}{1-x-a} & \frac{1-a}{1-x-a} & \frac{1-a}{1-x-a} & \frac{1-a}{1-x-a} & 0 & 0 \\ 0 & 0 & 0 & 1 & 0 & \frac{1}{1-s} & \frac{s}{1-s} \\ 0 & 0 & 0 & 0 & 0 & \frac{1}{1-s} & \frac{1}{1-s} \end{pmatrix}$$

If consumers and businesses behaved as postulated by Theory 6C, both the Federal Reserve and the private banks would be quite unable to influence the level of the national product. Moreover, the banking system would be unaffected by changes in consumer demand and the demand for plant. Because changes in the banking factors have no effect on the nonbank variables, and also changes in nonbank factors do not affect banking variables, the banking sector of the economy is effectively isolated from the rest of the economy.

Table 6.4. The Implications of Theory 6C

THE EFFECT OF A UNIT INCREASE IN	*The Effect upon*						
	NATIONAL PRODUCT	CONSUMPTION	INVESTMENT	NET WORTH	PLANT	MONEY	BANK LOANS
Consumer demand (ΔF_C)	$\frac{1}{1-x-a}$	$\frac{1-x}{1-x-a}$	$\frac{x}{1-x-a}$	$\frac{x}{1-x-a}$	$\frac{x}{1-x-a}$	0	0
Demand for plant (ΔF_K)	$\frac{1}{1-x-a}$	$\frac{a}{1-x-a}$	$\frac{1-a}{1-x-a}$	$\frac{1-a}{1-x-a}$	$\frac{1-a}{1-x-a}$	0	0
Supply of Loans (ΔR)	0	0	0	1	0	$\frac{1}{1-s}$	$\frac{s}{1-s}$
Excess reserves (ΔF_R)	0	0	0	0	0	$\frac{1}{1-s}$	$\frac{1}{1-s}$

All four of the theories presented in this chapter have one feature in common: Changes in consumer demand (F_C) and in the demand for plant (F_K) have no effect upon the banking system. Bank decisions about loans (and hence excess reserves) are made entirely without reference to the level of business activity. But bankers could not, in real life, afford to ignore business conditions. They must consider the likelihood that borrowers will be able to repay their debts. If the national income is low, we might expect banks to be less optimistic about this likelihood than in times when the national income is high. Theory 6D will take this possibility into account.

The easiest way of asserting that the banks look at business conditions in deciding how many loans to make is to say that

$$L = (1 - r)M + zY + F_L \qquad z > 0$$

where r is the reserve requirement. In this case, since $M = R + L$, the demand for loans is

$$M - R = (1 - r)M + zY + F_L$$

and therefore, the demand for bank reserves goes *down* as the national incomes rises:

$$R = rM - zY - F_L$$

$$= rM - zY + F_R$$

If $z = 0$, the formula reduces to that used in Tiny Model 4.

This theory is more complicated than any of the other variants studied in this chapter because it contains *four* coefficients (a, b, r, z) rather than three. It would be simple enough to suppress r in order to achieve a more simple theory, but the Federal Reserve requirements are so important in practice that serious objections could be made to any theory disregarding them.

If Theory 6A is modified so as to take this form of bank behavior into account, it becomes

$$(\mathbf{0}, \mathbf{F_C}, \mathbf{K_0}, \mathbf{0}, \mathbf{F_K}, \mathbf{R}, \mathbf{F_L})$$

$$= (\mathbf{Y}, \mathbf{C}, \mathbf{I}, \mathbf{W}, \mathbf{K}, \mathbf{M}, \mathbf{L}) \begin{pmatrix} 1 & -a & 0 & 0 & 0 & 0 & -z \\ -1 & 1 & 0 & 0 & 0 & 0 & 0 \\ -1 & 0 & -1 & 0 & 0 & 0 & 0 \\ 0 & 0 & 0 & 1 & -b & 0 & 0 \\ 0 & 0 & 1 & -1 & 1 & 0 & 0 \\ 0 & 0 & 0 & -1 & 0 & 1 & -s \\ 0 & 0 & 0 & 1 & 0 & -1 & 1 \end{pmatrix}$$

The inverse form of Theory 6D is

$$(\mathbf{Y}, \mathbf{C}, \mathbf{I}, \mathbf{W}, \mathbf{K}, \mathbf{M}, \mathbf{L}) = (\mathbf{0}, \mathbf{F_C}, \mathbf{K_0}, \mathbf{0}, \mathbf{F_K}, \mathbf{R}, \mathbf{F_L})$$

$$\begin{pmatrix} \frac{1}{1-a} & \frac{a}{1-a} & 0 & 0 & 0 & \frac{z(1-b)}{(1-a)(1-b)(1-s)} & \frac{z(1-b)}{(1-a)(1-b)(1-s)} \\ \frac{1}{1-a} & \frac{1}{1-a} & 0 & 0 & 0 & \frac{z(1-b)}{(1-a)(1-b)(1-s)} & \frac{z(1-b)}{(1-a)(1-b)(1-s)} \\ \frac{-1}{1-a} & \frac{a}{1-a} & -1 & 0 & 0 & \frac{-z(1-b)}{(1-a)(1-b)(1-s)} & \frac{-z(1-b)}{(1-a)(1-b)(1-s)} \\ \frac{b}{(1-a)(1-b)} & \frac{ab}{(1-a)(1-b)} & \frac{b}{1-b} & \frac{b}{1-b} & \frac{b}{1-b} & \frac{bz}{(1-a)(1-b)(1-s)} & \frac{bz}{(1-a)(1-b)(1-s)} \\ \frac{1}{(1-a)(1-b)} & \frac{a}{(1-a)(1-b)} & \frac{1}{1-b} & \frac{1}{1-b} & \frac{1}{1-b} & \frac{z}{(1-a)(1-b)(1-s)} & \frac{z}{(1-a)(1-b)(1-s)} \\ \frac{b}{(1-a)(1-b)} & \frac{ab}{(1-a)(1-b)} & \frac{b}{1-b} & \frac{1}{1-b} & \frac{1}{1-b} & \frac{bz+(1-a)(1-b)}{(1-a)(1-b)(1-s)} & \frac{bz+s(1-a)(1-b)}{(1-a)(1-b)(1-s)} \\ 0 & 0 & 0 & 0 & 0 & \frac{1}{1-s} & \frac{1}{1-s} \end{pmatrix}$$

The implications of Theory 6E are given in Table 6.5.

Theory 6D, then, states that if banks lend *more* as the national income rises, so that $z > 0$, then increases in consumer demand (F_C) and the demand for plant (F_K) increase the amount of money and of bank credit. This theory then implies that the banking sector is influenced by nonbank conditions.

One interesting application of this theory involves a little cheating. Usually we have treated all coefficients in our matrices as given numbers. Now suppose that z is not simply a given number, but that it changes according to the following rule:

(1) Banks have some estimate of what a proper, or "normal" level of the national product would be. Call this Y_N.
(2) If the national income is below Y_N, banks expect it to rise, and as it rises, they increase their loans. That is, $z > 0$, if $Y < Y_N$. If $Y = Y_N$, then $L = L_N$ is what banks consider to be a "normal" level of credit.
(3) If the national income is above Y_N, banks expect it to fall. As Y rises, they decrease their loans because they expect that borrowers will be caught by a recession and unable to repay. That is, $z < 0$ if $Y > Y_N$.

If this theory were true, when the national product went above Y_N, the money supply would start to drop. Literally, money would become "scarce" relative to goods, for all the other parts of the economy would continue to grow.

Actually, one of the things that has happened in all periods of prosperity since the second world war (1953, 1958, 1966, for example), is that it has become difficult for would-be borrowers to obtain loans. The amount of

Table 6.5. The Implications of Theory 6D

THE EFFECT OF A UNIT INCREASE IN	*The Effect upon*						
	NATIONAL PRODUCT	CONSUMPTION	INVEST-MENT	NET WORTH	PLANT	MONEY	BANK LOANS
Consumer demand (ΔF_C)	$\frac{1}{1-a}$	$\frac{1}{1-a}$	0	0	0	$\frac{z(1-b)}{(1-a)(1-b)(1-s)}$	$\frac{z(1-b)}{(1-a)(1-b)(1-s)}$
Demand for plant (ΔF_K)	$\frac{1}{(1-a)(1-b)}$	$\frac{a}{(1-a)(1-b)}$	$\frac{1}{1-b}$	$\frac{1}{1-b}$	$\frac{1}{1-b}$	$\frac{z}{(1-a)(1-b)(1-s)}$	$\frac{z}{(1-s)(1-b)(1-s)}$
Bank reserves (ΔR)	$\frac{b}{(1-a)(1-b)}$	$\frac{-ab}{(1-a)(1-b)}$	$\frac{b}{1-b}$	$\frac{1}{1-b}$	$\frac{b}{1-b}$	$\frac{bz+(1-a)(1-b)}{(1-a)(1-b)(1-s)}$	$\frac{bz+s(1-a)(1-b)}{(1-a)(1-b)(1-s)}$
Supply of loans (ΔF_L)	0	0	0	0	0	$\frac{1}{1-s}$	$\frac{1}{1-s}$

lending and credit do not actually decline, but they do not rise fast enough to satisfy borrowers. The Federal Reserve System has usually been blamed for this situation. The System usually replies that it is not to blame—it is not doing anything. This response is literally true. It does not satisfy the critics who say that if the System is doing nothing, then it should be doing something.

If, in fact, z changed sign in the manner suggested, there would exist a theory which explained why money became scarce when the national income rose "too much." This theory does not fully explain the "tight money" phenomenon: Businesses complain in periods of tight money that they actually must reduce investment. In Theory 6D, z does not appear in the first five columns of Table 6.5, so this effect would not occur. But the fact that we have $1/(1 - a)$ positive, and $z(1 - b)$ negative if $Y > Y_N$ suggests that one could develop a "tight money theory," for instance, by putting $-z$ in place of a zero in row 1, column 7 of the matrix of Theory 6B.

SUMMARY AND CONCLUSIONS

This chapter has set forth the simplest theories involving the national product, nonbank balance sheets, and bank balance sheets. These theories are all based on the following social accounting scheme:

1. The national product *equals* consumption plus investment.
2. Nonbank assets consist of money and plant; the nonbank liabilities side of the balance sheet consists of bank loans and net worth.
3. Investment is the change in plant.
4. Bank assets consist of reserves and loans; bank liabilities consist of money (checking accounts).

There are seven variables to be accounted for, and in addition to the four accounting definitions, it was necessary to supply statements describing the behavior of:

5. Households (as buyers of consumer goods).
6. Businesses (as buyers of plant).
7. Banks (as lenders, and by inference, as holders of bank reserves).

These simple theories do not mention government, the bond market, or the interest rate explicitly. They are the barest skeleton of an economy. However, all theories are emphatically about the same economy, and their differences can be stated precisely (Table 6.6.)

Table 6.6. Comparison of the Assumptions in Theories 6A to 6D

THEORY	CONSUMER SPENDING DEPENDS ON	BUSINESS DEMAND FOR PLANT DEPENDS ON	BANK SUPPLY OF LOANS DEPENDS ON
6A	Income	Assets	Money
6B	Money	Money	Money
6C	Income	Income	Money
6D	Income	Net worth	Money and income

The four theories presented do not exhaust all the possible permutations and combinations that could be prepared, but they do have rather different implications. In each theory, these are the same four independent factors: consumer demand (F_C), business demand for plant (F_K), bank reserves (R), which are assumed to be determined by Federal Reserve action, and the level of supply of loans (F_L), which is the "opposite" of the demand for excess reserves ($F_L = -F_R$, in terms of Tiny Model 4). Table 6.7 is a comparison of these four theories in one particular respect. It shows the theories for which a particular variable is affected by each of the four factors in the system.

Each theory given here involves three behavioral statements and coefficients.[1] But the conclusions reached are different. To claim that one of these theories applies to the United States in 1968, a selection must be made. For Theory 6B implies that the supply of bank loans affects the national income,

Table 6.7. Comparison of the Implications of Theories 6A to 6D

	Theories in which the given variable is affected by changes in the listed factor						
CHANGES IN	NATIONAL PRODUCT	CONSUMPTION	INVESTMENT	NET WORTH	PLANT	MONEY	BANK LOANS
Consumer demand (F_C)	All	All	C	C	C	D	D
Demand for plant (F_K)	All	Not B	All	All	All	D	D
Bank reserves (R)	Not C	Not C	Not C	All	Not C	All	All
Supply of loans (F_L)	B	B	B	B	B	All	All

[1] Actually Theory 6D had four coefficients. We could, however, suppress the fourth—reserve requirements—so that bank loans did not depend on reserves, and did not alter the present conclusions.

and the others do not. Theory 6D implies that consumer demand and the demand for plant affect commercial banks, and the others do not. Theory 6C implies that consumer demand affects investment, and the others do not. Then the implications of the alternatives consider the following possibilities: Either the supply of loans affects the national income, or it does not. If it does, 6B is the relevant theory, and the others are not. Either consumer demand and the demand for plant affect the banks, or they do not. If they do, 6D is the relevant theory and the others are not. Either consumer demand affects business investment or it does not. If it does, 6C is the relevant theory, and the others are not.

Again, suppose there is an increase of $1.00 in autonomous demand for plant, F_K. According to 6A, the national product will increase by $1/(1 - a)$; 6B states it will increase by 1; 6C states that it will increase by $1/(1 + x - a)$; and 6D states that it will increase by $1/(1 - a)$. These numbers are all different, and even if $1/(1 - a) > 1$, it may be that $1/(1 + x - a) < 1$. Consequently, the prediction about the effect of an increase in the demand for plant is by no means independent of the behavioral assumptions made in the theory.

In this chapter, economic theory has made several proposed explanations of economic life. They are rather different proposals, and within the domain of economic theory it is not possible to prove that one of them is more relevant to a discussion of (say) the United States economy of the 1970s than the others.

This conclusion is a particularly important one for readers of economic theory textbooks to remember. Theorists have a tendency to feel that their theory is relevant because it has been worked out properly. Many textbook writers suggest that the answers to practical questions—including questions of government policy—can be decided on purely abstract grounds merely because the assumptions made are plausible ones.

Table 6.7 is a handy first step to test the generality of conclusions reached on purely abstract grounds. For example, a change in the level of consumer demand (F_C) affects the national product in all four theories. There are 10 noncontroversial statements of this sort derivable from Table 6.7

Unfortunately, the list of noncontroversial statements is not a very exciting one. In particular, it does not include the statements about government policy that most of us would like to make. To illustrate, let us ask whether increases in government spending or additions to bank reserves will increase consumption. This is an important practical question.

Let us suppose, to simplify matters, that we have decided that Theory 2 is valid. Then government spending affects the economy just as does investment. Now we turn to Table 6.6 Increases in government spending (it says) will increase consumption unless Theory 6B holds. Increases in bank reserves will increase consumption unless Theory 6C holds. Thus changes in government spending have the same effect on consumption as do changes in bank reserves if either 6A or 6D is valid. Government spending will *not* affect consumption if consumer and business demand depends only on cash balances; bank reserves will *not* affect consumption if consumer and business demand depends solely on income and not on cash or total assets.

Thus Table 6.7 shows that the ability of a government policy to achieve a desired objective depends on the way consumers, businesses, and banks respond to changes in their incomes and assets. Theory alone does not tell us how they will act. It says only that if they act in a specific way, W, the effect will be some particular, E. Thus theory tells us the implications of the various behavior patterns. It is up to the economic historians and statisticians to tell us how, in fact, consumers, businesses, and banks have behaved.

Problems for Chapter 6

Readers are especially urged to work out the following problems. The four versions of Theory 6 require some careful thought, and problems are the most direct way to master their implications.

Problem 1 Theory 6A says a \$1.00 increase in bank reserves will increase the national product by $b/(1-a)(1-b)$; Theory 6B says the increase will be $(w+v)/(1-s)$. Compare the different reactions of consumers and of businesses which explain the differences in result. Why is it that s does not appear in the first expression, even though s appears in Theory 6A?

Problem 2 Theory 2 shows that under certain conditions an increase in government spending has the same effect on the economy as an increase in investment. Would that conclusion necessarily hold in the context of Theory 6?

Problem 3 Suppose that government spending is used exclusively to build bridges, roads, and other "productive assets," and that the conditions of Theory 2 apply. Then government spending acts on the economy in the same way as investment. Suppose that an increase in national product equal to ΔY is sought, and this increase may be obtained either by increasing government spending or by increasing bank reserves. Compare the magnitudes of the two which would be needed (a) under conditions of Theory 8A; (b) under conditions of Theory 6B.

Problem 4 The "multiplier" of Tiny Model 1 and Theory 6A says that if investment increases by \$1.00 the national product rises by $1/(1-a)$. In Theory 6C the corresponding multiplier is $1/(1-x-a)$. Which of the two is larger? How do you account for the difference?

Problem 5 Compare the efficacy of changes in government spending and in Federal Reserve policy as a means of affecting the national product in Theory 6C.

Problem 6 Suppose Theory 6D is valid, and that the interest rate is (for some reason) fixed. Suppose Federal Reserve wishes to stabilize bank credit as a means of stabilizing the earnings of the commercial banks. What will it do to offset the effects of $1.00 decreases in consumer demand (F_C) and the demand for plant (F_K).

Problem 7 At the beginning of this chapter, Theories 6A–6D were characterized in terms of the "influences" exerted by the various sectors upon the workings of the economy. Compare these characterizations with the Tables giving their respective implications, and give a precise definition of statements of the form "Sector *X* influences Sector *Y*."

Problem 8 Bankers are never very popular, because everyone owes them money. But there are two current views about the commercial banks. (1) Money is indeed the root of all evil, and the banks are able to manipulate all economic affairs to their own ends. (2) Banks are really quite passive creatures, whose function is merely to respond to the changing needs which business has for money. Use Tables 6.6 and 7.6 to cast light on the conditions in which each of these views is defensible.

Problem 9 Under what conditions can a country devise some combination of changes in government spending and bank reserves which will hold the national income constant, increase investment, and decrease consumption. (This is a common objective of underdeveloped countries.)

7

NATIONAL INCOME, THE GENERAL WELFARE, AND PUBLIC POLICY

CONTROL OVER ECONOMIC ACTIVITY

The list of *factors* in the various versions of Theory 6 consisted of: the level of consumer demand (F_C), the level of demand for plant (F_K), the level of the supply of loans (F_L), and bank reserves (R). The factors in earlier theories were frequently related to these. For instance, Theory 1 spoke of the demand for investment, rather than the demand for plant. But some additional elements of importance appeared there. For instance, government spending (F_G) and "property taxes" (F_T) appeared in Theories 2 and 3. Generally speaking, a *factor* is associated with some behavioral characteristic of a particular collection of economic units. The whole point of calculating the inverse form of an economic theory is to show how a change in each of these independent forms of behavior will change each of the variables in the economy. Our theory may involve only a few forms of economic activity, or it may involve a great many. Whatever its scope and degree of detail, changes in the system are brought about by changes in the factors.

As we all know, people are frequently dissatisfied with the way the economy works. To some extent, this dissatisfaction takes the form, "Why should Joe be so rich while I am so poor?" This type of dissatisfaction is not readily handled by the analysis in this book. But historically, there have been basic elements of macroeconomic displeasure. For instance:

(1) In the 1880s and 1890s the question was asked, "Why must all prices be declining?"

(2) In the 1930s the question was asked, "Why must so many people be unable to find work?"
(3) In the 1940s and 1960s the question was asked, "Why must all prices be rising?"
(4) Over all of this period, the question is asked, "Why is it that some years business conditions are good and in other years they are bad? Can't things be evened out a bit?"

When large groups of people ask such questions, the "Why" is not a matter of intellectual curiosity. It means, "We don't like this fact, and we want something done about it."

The theorist may say that the difficulties suggested by (1) and (2) mean that one or more of the factors in the economy ought to be increased; (3) means that one or more factors ought to be decreased; (4) means that one or more factors ought to be kept from changing.

But most of the factors involve large groups of economic units. To say that F_C is "too small" means that somehow, one must persuade all consumers to spend more, from any given income. To say that F_K is "too small" means that one must persuade businesses that they really want more plant. Tasks of this sort are essentially hopeless because there is no way to proceed. Advertisers, for example, are to some degree successful in persuading buyers to buy Brand *Y* rather than Brand *X* toothpaste. But they are not visibly successful in making people buy more of both Brand *X* and Brand *Y*. In part this lack of success reflects lack of interest. No individual business has an interest in financing a campaign, such as "Buy more goods." Although he does finance campaigns, the businessman means, "Buy more from me."

It is, of course, true that attitudes of consumers, businesses, and banks change over time. If they did not, the complaints made about the economy would always be the same, which they are not. The only complaint common to all periods is (4)—things keep changing. But these changes seem to be spontaneous and uncontrollable.

There are, in fact, only two economic units that are big enough to influence the entire economy, and hence so big that maybe they could counteract the influences of the other factors in the economy. Both of these economic units are part of the Federal Government. They are the tax collection and spending system which make up the Federal Government Budget[1] and the "bank for bankers," the Federal Reserve System. It is natural for people who are dissatisfied at any moment with the macroeconomic workings of the economy

[1] It is important to distinguish between the Federal Government and all government. There are, after all, fifty state governments and several thousand local governmental units, all of which collect taxes and spend money. It is at least as difficult to obtain concerted action by the states, and by local governments as it would be to obtain concerted action by comparable groups of business organizations. But there is only one Federal Government, and it is very large.

to turn to one or both of these economic units to remedy their complaints.

It is natural, then, to ask what the Federal Government could achieve by fiscal policy (the deliberate control of spending and taxation) or by monetary policy (the deliberate control of the level of bank reserves) as a means of influencing the variables in the economy. This is a question that has long interested economists and the general public. In the case of monetary policy, the discussion goes back at least as far as the Napoleonic Wars (which ended in 1815). The Bank of England, which is the English counterpart of the Federal Reserve System, was accused of being responsible for wartime inflation and postwar depression in that period. Monetary theory, in considerable degree, is the result of the very serious study undertaken at that time by English economists. The discussion of fiscal policy, in contrast, is mainly the result of the study of the depression of the 1930s; this depression was worldwide, but the analysis used here was developed mainly in Britain and the United States. It is only comparatively recently (in the 1950s) that the balance sheet analysis used in monetary economics has been combined with the income analysis used in fiscal policy analysis, and a good deal still remains to be done.

OPTIMAL POLICIES

Discussions of fiscal and monetary policies involve many issues that are not, properly speaking, macroeconomic. There is a basic general problem in economics as to how an economy will operate (a) in the absence of government intervention, and (b) if there is government intervention.

This problem might be illustrated in the macroeconomic context of Theory 3. In the economy described by that theory, assume that some minimal amount of government spending, F_G, is for good purposes, and that some tax system, $T = tY + F_T$ is defensible. (It might be that $F_G = F_T = t = 0$, for instance.) Now, given the other factors in the economy (F_C and F_I), we can find out what values the variables in the economy will be. That is, we can find a vector $\mathbf{V}_1 = (\mathbf{Y}, \mathbf{C}, \mathbf{T}, \mathbf{G}, \mathbf{I})$. If the actual level of government spending is F_G' and the actual tax system is describable by $T = t'Y + F_T'$, then the variables in the economy will be represented by the vector

$$\mathbf{V}_2 = (\mathbf{Y}', \mathbf{C}', \mathbf{T}', \mathbf{G}', \mathbf{I}').$$

Which of these two vectors is "better"? Does it make any sense to ask such a question?

In this theory, C measures the final goods going to households and I measures the final goods going to businesses. Suppose $C' > C$ and, also, $I' > I$. In this case, V_2 leaves both households and businesses "better off," since each receives more if V_2 is the case than if V_1 is the case. Therefore, V_1 is certainly not an optimal policy.

But suppose $C' > C$ and $I' < I$. In this case, as we go from V_1 to V_2, we "give" goods to households and "take" goods from businesses. If we wanted to state that "the economy" as a whole is better off, we would have to be prepared to prove that the gains of consumers exceeded, in some sense, the losses of businesses.

Suppose we consider all possible levels of government spending and taxes. For each level, G_0, T_0 (if Theories 2 or 3 are valid), there is a vector $(\mathbf{Y}_0, \mathbf{C}_0, \mathbf{F}_0, \mathbf{G}_0, \mathbf{I}_0)$ representing the consequence of G_0, T_0 on the economy. We shall call G_0, T_0 an *optimal policy* if, when we consider any alternative, such as G', T', we cannot find $C' > C_0$ and $I' > I_0$. That is, if G_0, T_0 is optimal there is no way to find a different policy which makes everyone better off.[2]

[*Parenthesis.* Some economists who read this section will object to the notion that I is to be thought of as a quantity of goods going to businesses. They will claim that we can think of the welfare of owners of businesses, the welfare of employees of businesses, or the welfare of managers of businesses, but we cannot meaningfully define the welfare of business, apart from people associated with it. However, these economists will reach exactly the same definition of *optimal policy* in the following way. Investment (they will say) increases tomorrow's productive capacity and hence tomorrow's income. If $C' > C_0$ and $I' > I_0$, then policy G', T' makes it possible for people to have more goods today and also more goods tomorrow than policy G_0, T_0. Hence G_0, T_0 is not optimal. However, if $C' > C_0$, and $I' < I_0$, the only way of obtaining more goods today (going from C_0 to C') is by giving up goods tomorrow (going from I_0 to I'). The next section will take this matter up in more detail.]

DECISION PROCESSES AND OPTIMAL POLICIES

The definition of *optimal policy* seems backward at first. A policy is not optimal if there is another policy which would leave everyone better off. If Peter and Paul are roommates, and both prefer to study with a television set going, then it is not an optimal policy for the set to be turned off, assuming that an optimal policy must be satisfactory to Peter, to Paul, and to nobody else. To justify leaving the television set off, it is necessary to assert that there is someone who knows better than Peter and Paul what is good for them.

[2] The term *optimal* as defined here is sometimes replaced by the term *Pareto-optimal*, after the Italian economist Vilfredo Pareto (1848–1923). This word is used as a technical term, and readers should not interpret it as meaning anything that is not implied by the definition.

If the set is turned on, the two roommates have a choice between two channels. Suppose Peter prefers Channel A to Channel B, and Paul prefers Channel B to Channel A. Then if the machine is switched from A to B, Peter is made worse off; if it is switched from B to A, Paul is made worse off. In other words, both Channel A and Channel B are optimal programs. The set should clearly be on, not off; it should be tuned either to Channel A or to Channel B; there is no way to say which of these channels is best.

If an economic process does not lead to an "optimal result," this means that there would be a way to make everyone better off, after the process had worked itself out. In the case above, imagine that Peter and Paul have agreed not to turn the television set on until they have decided which channel to listen to. This decision is not optimal, for it has been specified that both prefer to work with the set going. Whichever channel is selected, there is nobody who would rather have the set turned off; and there is somebody who is listening to his favorite channel. In this example, it is not optimal to leave the set off until a decision is reached about the channel. An optimal policy might be the following: Turn the set on. Decide the channel tentatively by flipping a coin. Then argue.

Thus, there are two elements involved in analyzing policy questions: (1) describing the characteristics of optimal policies in a particular case; and (2) describing the process by which decisions are reached. In the example, either Channel A or Channel B is optimal. Having the set off is not optimal; having the set tuned to any channel other than A and B is not optimal. In the example, it is suggested that flipping a coin is a way to reach some optimal policy. Another way of deciding would be to measure the biceps of Peter and of Paul, and to let the man with the larger biceps choose. A third way would be to let Peter bribe Paul to listen to Peter's favorite program.

Theories in this book are mainly about economic processes. But since government agencies appear in the theories as purchasers of goods and services and (in the case of Federal Reserve) bonds, it is necessary to distinguish two kinds of decision processes. In most economic processes, there is some reason to believe that outcomes will be optimal, in the special sense given above. If Peter has some automobiles and Paul has some money, Peter will swap an automobile for some money providing he gets enough money to make him feel better off; and Paul will make the swap providing he gets enough automobile to make him feel better off. A deal will take place whenever two people can be made better off. No deal will take place if one party would be made worse off in consequence; such a party would refuse to trade.

Suppose, however, that Peter and Paul have a neighbor who likes Channel C and dislikes Channels A and B. In this case, the decision reached by Peter and Paul will never be one which leaves the neighbor pleased. He may have to listen to Channels A and B, if the walls of the rooms are thin enough.

There is no reason to suppose that Peter and Paul will take the neighbor's likes and dislikes into account.

The analytical problems involved here are twofold. First, the actions taken by Peter and Paul influence not only their own welfare, but the neighbor's welfare. This fact changes the nature of optimal policies. Second, if three people are affected by policy decisions, but only two participate in the decisions, the result will not be the same as it would be if everybody participated.

If single decisions involve the participation of three or more people, they are "political" rather than "economic." It is no longer true that actions are taken if and only if *pairs* of persons are made better off. Instead, more complicated rules hold. In some cases, a majority may be required to reach a decision; in other cases unanimity. Political processes are different, even if they involve the purchase of goods and services by government. That is why political science and economics are different disciplines. That is also why government is mainly a "factor" rather than a "variable" in this book: Its actions are thought not to be determined in any simple way resembling the behavior of businesses and consumers.

FULL EMPLOYMENT AND OPTIMALITY

Suppose that the economy, left to itself, worked out the vector $\mathbf{V}_0 = (\mathbf{Y}_0, \mathbf{C}_0, \mathbf{T}_0, \mathbf{G}_0, \mathbf{I}_0)$. At this level of the national product, 5 percent of the labor force is unemployed. Now suppose this state of affairs annoys the electorate, and after an election, the new Congress changes government spending and taxes so as to produce the vector $\mathbf{V}' = (\mathbf{Y}', \mathbf{C}', \mathbf{T}', \mathbf{G}', \mathbf{I}')$, and 4 percent unemployment. If Theories 2 and 3 are valid, it is quite possible that $C' > C_0$ and also $I' > I_0$. Thus consumers and businesses all have more goods. In this case, it would seem that $\mathbf{V}_0$ is certainly inferior to $\mathbf{V}'$. That is, $\mathbf{V}_0$ is certainly not optimal, for there is a level of spending and taxes which leaves everyone better off than in $\mathbf{V}_0$.

The last paragraph employs a very common type of reasoning used to justify fiscal policies that have a tendency to reduce unemployment. While there is unemployment, the government, it is said, may increase spending in such a way as to leave everyone better off. However, if there is no unemployment, the government can increase its spending only if it has a way of taking goods away from others. In this sense, full employment is an optimal state of the economy, while a state in which there is unemployment is not. We shall now consider this proposition in more detail.

In periods of unemployment (by definition), there are people out of work. If these people could be put to work, there could perhaps be more goods both for businesses and for consumers. In this sense, the government could make everyone better off by taking action to decrease unemployment.

The allocation of the national product between consumption and investment has so far been thought of in terms of a division of goods between consumers and businesses. But there is another way of looking at this division—a way which is more common to economists. Investment is the *change* in plant in the economy. The level of productive capacity of the economy is partly determined by the *amount* of plant in the economy. If the economy always produced as many goods as it physically could (so that there was no unemployment), then the amount of investment would determine the rate of growth of output. The rate of growth of output determines the rate at which consumption can grow.

Therefore, when an economy decides, whether by market or political processes, how much investment shall take place, it also decides how rapidly consumption shall grow. Decisions about the relative shares of consumption and investment are in this sense decisions about the relative sizes of present and future consumption.

We may illustrate this proposition symbolically. In what follows, a subscript t refers to a date: Y_t, for instance, is the national product in year t.

Suppose that the economy is producing at capacity in year t. Then $Y_t = C_t + I_t$ is a constant total. If consumption changes, investment must change in the opposite direction: $0 = \Delta C_t + \Delta I_t$, so that $\Delta I_t = -\Delta C_t$.

Suppose also that the output of the economy depends on employment (N) and plant (K) in the following way:

$$Y_t = nN_t + kK_t + F_{N,t}$$

$$Y_{t+1} = nN_{t+1} + kK_{t+1} + F_{N,t+1}$$

and so on, for each year. Then, of course,

$$K_{t+1} = K_t + I_t$$

so that

$$Y_{t+1} = nN_{t+1} + kK_t + kI_t + F_{N,t+1}$$

If there is full employment and a constant labor force, N_{t+1} is a constant. At time $(t + 1)$, the amount of plant that existed at time t cannot be changed; and $F_{N,t+1}$ is also given. Hence Y_{t+1} varies with I_t:

$$\Delta Y_{t+1} = k\Delta I_t$$

and therefore

$$\Delta Y_{t+1} = -k\Delta C_t$$

Thus an increase in consumption at time t has the effect of decreasing income at time $(t + 1)$. If, as we have often assumed,

$$C_{t+1} = aY_{t+1} + F_{C,t+1}$$

then

$$\Delta C_{t+1} = -ak\Delta C_t + \Delta F_{C,t+1}$$

Because $-ak$ is negative, we are justified in saying that increases in consumption at time t mean decreases in potential consumption at time $(t + 1)$, *providing* that the economy works at full capacity.

Problem Suppose that government spending is taken into account, so that $Y = C + I + G$. Show that if the economy is always at full employment, an increase in government spending at time t means a reduction in $(C + I)$ at time $(t + 1)$.

The "gimmick" that makes this demonstration work, of course, is the assumption that the economy is always working at capacity. Usually, of course, there is some unemployed labor and some unutilized plant. If this is true, the proper statement of the foregoing result would be that increases in investment at time t mean increases in the ability of the economy to produce goods (including consumer goods) at time $(t + 1)$.

EXTERNAL EFFECTS OF FISCAL POLICY

So far, we have pretended that the welfare of households was determined solely by the amount of consumer goods they received (C), and that the welfare of businesses was determined solely by the amount of investment (I) they were able to undertake. It is not clear, when we look into the matter, that this pretense is justified.

Suppose we compare two vectors that are the same except with respect to government spending: $\mathbf{V}_1 = (\mathbf{C}, \mathbf{I}, \mathbf{G})$; $\mathbf{V}_2 = (\mathbf{C}, \mathbf{I}, \mathbf{G}')$. Can we really conclude that the welfare of households and businesses is the same, since C and I are the same in both cases?

In order to conclude anything about this question, we must make some assumption about the objects which the government buys. If, for example, the government builds roads for consumers to drag-race on, an increase in government spending will increase the welfare of drag-racers. In this case, the welfare of consumers is increased when government spending rises. If, for example, the government spends its money on wire-tapping devices, the welfare of telephone users will decrease.

These examples may seem odd ones. For instance, drag-racers tend to annoy the rest of the public. If the new roads built for them are used by other drivers, one revives the problem of robbing Peter to pay Paul. The installation of traffic lights and speed limits may please some people, but it annoys people who are in a hurry. The tapping of telephone lines certainly annoys those whose lines are tapped. If criminals are captured in consequence, their victims will be pleased. But criminal and noncriminal users of telephones are inconvenienced.

These examples are all cases of *externality*—the welfare of one person is affected by the actions of others as well as by his own actions. Businesses that dump wastes into rivers, that finance scholarships for people in their community, individuals who play the drums late at night, and so forth, are all engaged in actions that affect other people as well as themselves. In particular, much, perhaps most, government spending may be thought of in these terms.

Over half of all Federal Government spending in the late 1960s went for the armed forces, and a good deal of the military spending went into the war in Viet Nam. This spending had been approved by Congress, and as a political decision, had been approved by a majority of the population. On the other hand, if the armed forces had been supported by voluntary contributions, spending would have been much smaller. One part of the electorate felt that the war in Viet Nam was desirable, and that this spending was useful to all Americans. One part of the electorate felt that the war in Viet Nam was undesirable and that this spending was harmful to all Americans. From this point of view, if each individual is the best judge of what is good for him, this government spending would have benefited some and injured others.

As a practical matter, all governments and all societies say that some persons, in some respects, are not good judges of what is good for them. Most countries say that children should go to school, that young men should serve for a time in the armed forces, that people who commit certain actions should go to prison, and that people who commit other actions should go to mental hospitals. In all these respects, individuals are held to be bad judges of what is good for them. As a practical matter, all governments and all societies allow some choice to individuals. "Gentlemen prefer blondes" is a generalization (perhaps a false one), and has no legal status in the choice of mates.

If one were convinced that government spending always forced the community either (a) to divert resources from current consumption and investment, because the economy was ordinarily at full employment; or (b) to undergo externalities that made businesses and individuals worse off, one would always be opposed to increases in government spending.

If (a) were false, and the economy were not using all resources, then one might favor government spending as a means of increasing consumption and investment, provided one did not take the extreme conservative view about government spending which was outlined in Theory 3.

If both (a) and (b) were false, then increased government spending would increase the goods available for businesses and consumers, and might also have an external effect that would benefit both these groups. In the extreme case (for instance, in a war which everyone supports), an increase in government spending might benefit everyone, although it reduced the amount of goods available both to business and government.

WELFARE ASPECTS OF MONETARY POLICY

Even if one took the view that government spending always had undesired external effects, governmental action *other than* increased spending might still benefit the economy. In particular, the Federal Reserve System, by controlling bank reserves, can influence (in certain circumstances) the level of business and consumer spending, and hence the level of business and consumer welfare.

This last statement, like the statements made earlier about fiscal policy, relies upon theories presented earlier. Theories 6A, 6B, and 6D all show that when the Federal Reserve adds to member bank reserves, the national output rises; Theory 2 says that when government spending rises, the national output also rises. However, these statements are purely logical, and if the economy did not obey the rules laid down in the theories, they could not necessarily be derived. Thus, Theory 3 discussed theories in which increases in government spending would not necessarily increase the national product, and Theory 6C gives a case in which increases in bank reserves have no effect on the national product. Theorists must insist that they can (if they are clever) construct all sorts of "perverse" theories which would have to be shot down in flames by empirical economists before any theory could be proved relevant, say, to the United States economy of 1968.

However, let us suppose that the world is as described in 6A, 6B, or 6D. Then the Federal Reserve can influence the level of output *without* having the government buy goods which have "external effects." If government spending always had undesirable side effects, then government action in economic life would be limited to action by the Federal Reserve to control the level of bank reserves.

If Federal Reserve action can increase the level of national product, then there are certainly cases where it can make everyone better off. These are the cases where there is unemployment. But in cases where there is full employment, then, of course, the Federal Reserve may well, like the fiscal agencies, make some people better off and others worse off.

This statement may be considered from several points of view. First, Federal Reserve action affects the economy through the banking system, and the banking system affects the cash and the debts of the community. The debts of the community are mostly incurred for purposes other than current consumption: homebuilding, business expansion, and government spending. If there is full employment, and if the Federal Reserve carries on open market operations, then the immediate effect of these actions is mainly on investment. If reserves rise, investment goes up, and the amount of consumption may well decline. If reserves fall, investment declines, and consumption may well rise. In fact, the loudest criticisms of the Federal Reserve are ordinarily made when there is full employment.

Second, it was shown in Theory 5 that Federal Reserve actions can affect interest rates. In that theory, there was only one "visible" interest rate, which could be determined from knowledge of the market price of bonds, and conditions given on the face of the bonds. There was an "invisible" rate on bank loans, which could not be determined from the data in that theory. American capital markets include a great many different interest rates, for there are many kinds of borrowers and lenders, and many kinds of loan arrangements. The people active in these markets are convinced (from their experience) that when the Federal Reserve operates in the government bond market, it affects other interest rates as well as the interest rate on government bonds.

Whenever interest rates change, the welfare of borrowers and of lenders changes. When interest rates rise, lenders become better off and borrowers become worse off. Naturally there are many more borrowers than lenders, and when the market (with or without Federal Reserve aid) increases the interest rate, political reactions take place to urge the Federal Reserve to act so as to reduce the interest rate again.

In other words, the Federal Reserve System, like the fiscal agencies of the Federal Government, does have an influence on the national product and on the welfare of individual groups in the community. This influence is less obvious than that of government spending, simply because it is carried on through the bond markets, which most people know nothing about; in contrast, everyone becomes aware of large government spending programs.

Virtually all economists would agree that both the fiscal and the monetary authorities can have *some* effect on the economy. Virtually all economists agree that on some occasions it may be useful to have the government influence the economy in *some* degree. But the choice of agency to which individual economists would assign the task will vary. To some extent this choice depends on the kind of theory the economist may have: Those who favor Theory 3 will reach conclusions different from the advocates of Theory 2; and those who favor Theory 6C will not agree with others about the effects of Federal Reserve action. To some extent this choice depends upon the economist's estimate of whether government actions of particular kinds are beneficial or not. That is, the choice depends on the individual's political preferences. These we respect as part of any individual's beliefs, but they are not part of his professional competence.

WELFARE AND UNREGULATED ECONOMIES: AN ILLUSTRATION

Since this chapter deals with evaluations of government policies, it has consisted mostly of an analysis of the way in which political decision processes may lead to results different from those which market decision processes might reach. Therefore, it has been stressed that governmental intervention in the economy might well not promote the general welfare—in the special sense that it may produce a nonoptimal level and composition of income or wealth.

It is worth showing that the market elements of the economy, left to themselves, may also produce undesirable results. This demonstration follows naturally from any of the versions of Theory 6, as we shall see. All of these theories make use of the statement that $K = K_0 + I$, which asserts that investment is the same thing as the change in plant. This statement would not be realistic if the theories dealt with the national income accounts in detail. Investment in those accounts includes changes in inventory as well as changes in plant. It would not be a realistic statement unless it specifies some treatment of depreciation, for plant changes because of depreciation as well as because of investment. Still the definition has been a useful one, for it has provided the simplest possible link between the income and nonbank balance sheet accounts.

At successive periods of time, the numbers that are represented in the statement $K = K_0 + I$ would naturally change. For the years 1968, 1969, and 1970, for example, we would have

$$K_{1968} = K_{1967} + I_{1968}$$
$$K_{1969} = K_{1968} + I_{1969}$$
$$K_{1970} = K_{1969} + I_{1970}$$

In every theory containing K_0 as the ith component of its vector of factors, a comparison of the factors in these 3 years would yield

$$(\mathbf{F}_{1,1968} \cdots \mathbf{K}_{1967}, \mathbf{F}_{i+1,1968} \cdots \mathbf{F}_{n,1968})$$
$$(\mathbf{F}_{1,1969} \cdots \mathbf{K}_{1968}, \mathbf{F}_{i+1,1969} \cdots \mathbf{F}_{n,1969})$$
$$(\mathbf{F}_{1,1970} \cdots \mathbf{K}_{1969}, \mathbf{F}_{i+1,1970} \cdots \mathbf{F}_{n,1970})$$

Suppose that all other factors affecting the economy are constant, but investment takes place, so that $K_{1969} > K_{1968} > K_{1967}$. Then, as the amount of plant in the economy changes, the variables in the economy will also change. In this sense, the growth of the economy affects economic processes.

Roughly speaking, the reason for this phenomenon is the following: Suppose that businesses want some particular amount of plant, $\bar{K}$. To obtain it, they must supplement what they have, K_0, by new investments. The more plant they already have, the less they must buy to obtain what they want. The less they must buy, the less investment there will be, and therefore the less the national product will be.

This proposition may be stated more exactly. In Theories 6A to 6D, K_0 appears as a factor. The other factors were consumer demand (F_C), demand for plant (F_K), bank reserves (R), and the supply of loans (F_L). Suppose all of these other factors are fixed, and that in 1968 there is investment equal to I_{1968}. Then the economy in 1969 will be different from 1968 because (and only because) K_0 has changed. Moreover, $\Delta K_0 = I_{1968}$. The effect of this change on all the variables of the system is measured by the elements in row 3 of the inverse matrix of the four respective variants of the theory. These elements are given in Table 7.1. Obviously, if any investment takes place in period t, then, unless at least one factor rises in period $(t + 1)$, the level of economic activity will fall in period $(t + 1)$.

Suppose Theory 6A holds. Then if investment in period t is I_t, $\Delta K_{t+1} = I_t$, and $\Delta Y_{t+1} = [-1/(1 - a)]I_t$, if all other factors are constant. If Theory 6B holds, $\Delta Y_{t+1} = -I_t$, and so on. The magnitude of the decline varies from theory to theory, but a decline is nevertheless present in all of the theories.

Fiscal or monetary policies might remedy the declines in national product predicted by Table 7.1. Since Theory 6 is the basis for the present discussion, rather than a more complicated system, let us merely suppose that an argument about fiscal policy could be developed, if we put together a more complicated theory along the lines of Theory 2.

Increases in bank reserves, as noted in Chapter 6, may bring about increases in the national product. It is not certain that they do. Theory 6C says that the national product is not affected by bank reserves. But no plausible theory says that increases in bank reserves cause decreases in the national product. Therefore, let us throw aside caution, and suppose Theory 6C does not hold.

The other variants of Theory 6 all say that the more investment there is in period t, the more the national product falls in period $(t + 1)$. That is, the change in plant in period t is associated with changes in product in period $(t + 1)$. If the Federal Reserve wants to stabilize income, it must make changes in reserves proportional to changes in plant. That is, changes in reserves should be proportional to investment. The more investment there is in period t, the more reserves should be increased in period $(t + 1)$.

Now let us go back to the theory of fiscal policy. The discussion of Theory 2 led us to the conclusion that if the government wished to stabilize the national product, one way of doing so is to vary government spending so as to offset declines in investment. In other words, when investment falls, government spending should rise. When investment rises, government spending should fall.

Of course, the prescription of Theory 2 is almost exactly the opposite of that given in the preceding paragraph. One argument says that if investment

Table 7.1. Effect of one dollar's investment in period t upon the variables of the economy in period $(t + 1)$, according to Theories 6A to 6D.

	The Effect upon						
THEORY	NATIONAL PRODUCT	CONSUMPTION	INVESTMENT	NET WORTH	PLANT	MONEY	BANK LOANS
6A	$\frac{-1}{1-a}$	$\frac{-a}{1-a}$	-1	0	0	0	0
6B	-1	0	-1	0	0	0	0
6C	$\frac{-1}{1-x-a}$	$\frac{-a}{1-x-a}$	$\frac{-(1-a)}{1-x-a}$	$\frac{-x}{1-x-a}$	$\frac{-x}{1-x-a}$	0	0
6D	$\frac{-1}{1-a}$	$\frac{a}{1-a}$	-1	0	0	$\frac{-z}{(1-a)(1-s)}$	$\frac{-z}{(1-a)(1-s)}$

rises in period t, reserves and/or government spending should *rise* in period $(t + 1)$; the other says that if investment rises in period t, reserves and/or government spending should *fall* in period $(t + 1)$. We have to say "almost," because one argument relates to time period t, the other to period $(t + 1)$.

Should bank reserves rise or fall, when investment rises, if the economy is to be stabilized?

This question is a useful one to ask, for a variety of reasons. First, as theorists, it tells us that our theory is not really complete. In particular, it has not taken into account problems of timing. Instead of merely asking "Is there a proper *level* of government spending at a particular moment?" one should perhaps ask, "Is there a proper *schedule* of government spending to offset the consequence of some anticipated *schedule* of investment over a period of time?" This question relates to economic *dynamics*, or the way the economy behaves over periods of time. Dynamic theories take time systematically into account. They are inherently more difficult than those discussed in this book. Readers who have followed the reasoning of Theory 6 will understand why dynamic problems come up, even if they do not know how to construct dynamic theories.

This question also enables us to understand the difference between theoretical economists and applied economists. The theoretical economist will think: "Aha, I need a theory in which time plays a part. Presumably, I should not think of bank reserves as a number R, but as something which varies with time, $R(t)$; and I want a time pattern for $R(t)$ which will leave Y a constant (or maybe increasing at a steady rate). Is there any $R(t)$ with this property?"

The applied economist will think along different lines. Suppose, for example, that he is advising the Federal Reserve System. Then he will use a theory such as Theory 6B as a guide, but as nothing more. This theory tells him to buy when the national product is falling so as to offset the decline, or to sell if it is rising "too fast." A theory such as Theory 5 will tell him what to do *if* he wants certain changes in interest rates. But he does not need to know the numerical values of the coefficients in the theories (a, b, s, x, z, and so on). He does not have to know whether the coefficients are changing. He judges when to start (and stop) making purchases by looking directly at the variables in the economy. In the particular example under discussion, the dynamic process underlying changes may not particularly matter to central bankers.

It is of scientific interest to know what the numerical values of the coefficients of a theory may be, and how they have changed. But for many practical purposes, these coefficients are "only" of scientific interest. Applied economists can frequently work quite effectively with rather bad theories, simply because the defects in the theory are not (at the moment) of practical importance. It may be more important, in practical terms, to have up-to-date information and to be able to recognize changes in the economic situation promptly than it is to have a correct theory. But there are certainly times when unexpected events take place; and then the practical men turn to theorists for help.

Let us return to Table 7.1 and consider depreciation (a subject on which very little has been said). If some fraction d of plant wears out during the period, then in period t, depreciation will be dK_t; if I_t of new plant is bought during this period, then the increase in plant is given by $\Delta K_{t+1} = I_t - dK_t$. In this case

$$\Delta Y_{t+1} = \frac{-1}{1-a}(I_t - dK_t)$$

for Theory 6A. The more rapidly plant depreciates, the greater d will be, and the less the decline in income resulting from a given investment program. Indeed, if investment is represented as a rate of growth in plant ($I_t = eK_t$), then

$$\Delta Y_{t+1} = \frac{-(e-d)}{1-a} K_t = \frac{d-e}{1-a} K_t$$

For any given plant K_t, the greater d is, and the less e is, the smaller will be the fall in Y. For any given values of a, d, and e, the greater K_t, the greater will be the drop in Y in period $(t+1)$.

This conclusion has clear social welfare implications. In Theories 6A, 6C, and 6D, both households (C) and businesses (I) are worse off, so everyone is worse off. In Theory 6B, businesses are worse off and households are not better off, so social welfare can be said to have dropped. Therefore, these theories all mean that if investment is positive in period t, after allowance for depreciation, then welfare will decline in period $(t+1)$.

Observe that this result is not stated as an observed fact, but rather as a theoretical prediction. It is an example of a certain number of gloomy propositions in economics, which have led it to be called the "dismal science" by Carlyle. Carlyle was talking, of course, about another gloomy proposition by Thomas Malthus—perhaps the most famous of its kind. Malthus said in the early 1800s that if the population started off from a level of P_0 and grew at a *rate* of r per year for t years, it would be $P_0(1+r)^t$. If the food supply started off from a level of F_0, and grew by an amount of f per year, then at the end of t years it would be $F_0 + ft$. The food supply per person would be

$$\frac{F}{P} = \frac{F_0 + ft}{P_0(1+r)^t}$$

The larger t becomes, the less F/P will be, so that eventually we will all be at the brink of starvation.

This proposition led Malthus to advocate birth control, and his opponents suffered greatly. However, the main objection to Malthus' theory is that it is not true. In fact, food production has not grown more slowly than population over the past few centuries. Only in recent years have demographers been able to point to a real danger of food shortages for the world; and even here, the imbalance is concentrated in Latin America and certain parts of Asia.

Even if Malthus' theory is wrong, it has been extremely useful in stimulating thought and discussion on an interesting question. As a historical matter, the theory just propounded is also wrong. Even so, we may learn something about the power and limitations of economic theory by looking at it a little more closely.

AN INTRODUCTION TO SOME UNSOLVED PROBLEMS

In Table 7.1, it was shown that whatever variant of Theory 6 was considered, an increase in plant in period t led to a decrease in national product in period $(t + 1)$. Of course, this particular factor is not the only factor in the theory. If the levels of consumption (F_C), demand for plant (F_K), bank reserves (R), or supply of loans (F_L) increased, the decrease brought about by the increase in plant (K_0) might be offset. But the whole point of our classification of objects into factors and variables was to list those things (the factors) which could be considered capable of independent variation. It is a certain form of cheating if now we supplement our theory to say that these factors vary in such a way as to offset changes in plant. Why should they?

To explain why the factors should, or rather why they might change in such a way, is to introduce a bit more depth into theories than we have so far had. All of the theories thus far considered have been most useful in talking about month-to-month and year-to-year changes. But Table 7.1 raises a big historical problem: We look at the world today and compare it with the world in 1900. Obviously our cities and our factories have grown enormously in numbers and in size. Our farms now use vast amounts of machinery. Plant, which is K_0 in Theory 6, has grown tremendously. If Theory 6 were correct, income should have dropped enormously since 1900. Since it has not dropped, should we discard Theory 6?

The answer to this question is simple: Of course we should drop Theory 6, when we have a better one to take its place. But it is not easy to construct new and better theories. This book is designed for beginning students in macroeconomics. For this reason, we leave the more difficult subjects for more advanced courses. It is possible, nevertheless, to speak in a simple way about what a more satisfactory theory would have to explain. As it turns out, this discussion gives some ideas about what happens when an economy like the American economy turns from being a rural to an urban society, and when it absorbs a vast increase in knowledge, such as that which has taken place during the course of this century.

Decreases in national product are associated with decreases in employment. Why didn't the vast increase in American plant after 1900 bring about an enormous increase in unemployment? As a matter of fact, from one point of view, this is just what happened. When a business reduces its output, it may either lay some workers off, or make all workers work shorter hours. In 1900, American workers had a 60-hour week and in the 1960s, a 40-hour week. This reduction in employment is "as if" one third of the 1900 labor force had been discharged, but the social effects distributed among everyone.

In 1900, most children left school after a few years. In the 1960s, most children completed high school. In 1900 fewer people lived till age 65, but those who did continued to be employed. In the 1960s, most people of age 65 and over were retired on some sort of pension.

In other words, one of the predictions of Table 7.1 is not wrong. The increase in American plant has in fact reduced employment very considerably. It has not produced hardship, because mainly people have been willing to stay in school longer, to work shorter hours, and to retire sooner than formerly. Is this rise in "laziness" a good thing? It has certainly avoided the problems associated with unemployment.

When Table 7.1 was discussed, it was shown that not all investment decreased income, but only "net" investment—the difference between total construction of new plant and depreciation on existing plant. If one could imagine that whenever investment increased, there was a corresponding increase in the wearing out of plant, it would be impossible to increase the amount of plant in existence. Why might this sort of thing come about?

The theories in this book have associated the demand for plant with the demand for investment, since investment is the same thing as the change in plant. But can there be an economic event which causes business to say, "I do not necessarily want more plant than formerly, but I do want to tear down Factory A and build Factory B in its place?" If such decisions could be made, then investment today would not decrease income tomorrow, as Table 7.1 says it should.

The sort of decision described does occur whenever an invention is put to economic use. Such events are called *innovations*. Usually, an innovation introduces a new kind of output or a new kind of process. The accounting system used here does not report innovations. It merely says that new goods will either be part of consumption, part of investment, or part of government purchases. Moreover, the business that introduces a new product may have no intention of tearing down any factory buildings itself; indeed, it may be a new firm with no old assets. But of course, if the new firm is making something better than what was available formerly, the effect may be to close down older firms. From the economy's point of view, the innovation meant setting up a new factory and knocking down an old factory. Moreover, from the economy's point of view, the "old factory" that is knocked down is not necessarily of exactly the same size as the new factory. It might be "larger" or "smaller."

The statements about consumption that are made in the various theories considered in this book all consist of two parts. (1) Consumption is said to vary with income, or cash balances, or wealth. (2) Consumption is autonomous, that is, simply independent of anything else. In this sense, the term F_C appearing in all the statements about consumption is a measure of the standard of living Americans "insist upon" whether they can "afford" it or not. The circumstances in which Americans live are very different today from those of 1900. Houses are no longer simply large, waterproof boxes, but rather containers for considerable amounts of complicated machines that replace the labor of domestic servants, and even alter the climate of the dwelling. Today Americans are notoriously devoted to automobiles, in a way that seems to be independent of income or wealth. In 1900 they were not. This list of twentieth-century changes could be multiplied. It seems to amount to a long list of reasons why F_C is larger than it used to be. To some extent, these changes in F_C have to do with scientific advance. As new products have been introduced into the economy, consumer demand has changed. If this view is correct, then scientific advance is something that affects both consumers and businesses. But in the earlier discussions, F_C and F_K, or F_C and F_I were thought of as being quite independent of each other. Perhaps this view is too simple.

Finally, the various versions of Theory 6 all list bank reserves as an independent factor. (Other theories have listed government spending and tax rates as independent factors.) This way of treating government makes sense if we want to isolate the response pattern of the economy, so as to examine it. In principle, government agencies operate in quite different ways from businesses. When we treat these agencies as "factors" rather than as "variables" we merely recognize this fact.

But look back to the simplest version of the theory of money: $MV = PQ$. If the economy is growing, then Q is increasing. If savings tend to decline, as is suggested by the increase in consumption (F_C), then V will tend to rise. But it may well be that V does not rise as fast as Q. In this case, unless the quantity of money (M) rises, prices (P) will fall. It seems to be a well-established political fact that the community objects to falling prices.

Problem Explain why people who have debts may be worse off if their incomes and the prices of goods decline proportionately.

If the conditions of the last paragraph hold, then we may regard the Federal Reserve System as under pressure to expand bank reserves as growth takes place. If the System does not, then prices may fall, and political difficulties may arise. But to say this is to say that this government agency (and perhaps other government agencies, also) are not really independent factors. Perhaps much of their activity is merely a response to changes in the environment. It is certainly true that in the early 1930s, increased government spending took place because the government "had to" do something about the unemployed. President Hoover, in fact, was defeated in the election of 1932 because he had evidently "not done enough." Later presidents have been much more attentive to economic conditions, and in fact an act passed in 1946 created a Council of Economic Advisors to the President to try to make sure that the government would respond to changes in economic conditions.

Theory 6 was an improvement over the earlier theories in the book, in the sense that it combines income, asset, and banking system accounts into a single theory. In this sense it is "complete," although it is less detailed than the "sectoral" theories such as those dealing with fiscal policy, the banking system, and so on. The great virtue of such a complete theory is that it enables one to determine separately the influences of the consumer, business, banking, and Federal Reserve sectors on all parts of the economy. Moreover, the structure of Theory 6 is so flexible that a variety of behavior patterns can be examined. Since a theory can be accepted or rejected only on the basis of evidence, it is very useful to have a basic theoretical system that is consistent with a variety of possible behavior patterns which might turn out to exist in a particular historical context. The results of applying these various patterns seem plausible when a variety of historical events are considered.

But Theory 6, like any macroeconomic theory, has defects that turn up under closer scrutiny. In particular, it does not seem altogether plausible to predict that in an economy where plant grows rapidly, income will fall rapidly. Certainly this has not happened in twentieth-century America. To get round this difficulty, we would have to assume that the various factors in this theory are not independent of each other. But it is not easy to see exactly what sort of theory can tie them together, as long-run historical evidence suggests we should.

This book ends in a spirit consistent with its beginning. It has been possible both to expand upon simple theories and to combine simple theories. Thus, the book has shown how to incorporate complexities into a very simple view of macroeconomic events. If a claim were made that all of macroeconomics has been presented, the reader could conclude that macroeconomics is a dead subject. In fact, there is a good deal that has not even been mentioned. But readers who understand how to take the first steps undertaken in this book will have a way to go on to more difficult subjects. In particular, they will have some standards that tell them when they have an explanation for some collection of events, and when they do not.

SUGGESTED REFERENCES

(Textbooks are marked with an asterisk)

Social Accounting

Board of Governors of the Federal Reserve System, *Flow of Funds in the U.S. 1939–1953*. Washington, 1955.

Copeland, Morris A., *A Study of Moneyflows in the United States*. New York: National Bureau of Economic Research Inc., 1952.

Federal Reserve Bulletin, see Revision of Flow of Funds Accounts, Nov. 1965 for current flow of funds data.

National Bureau of Economic Research, *A Critique of the U.S. Income and Product Accounts*, Studies in Income and Wealth, vol. 22. Princeton, N.J. 1958.

Office of Business Economics, *U.S. Income and Output*. Washington, D.C.: Government Printing Office, 1959.

*Rosen, Sam, *National Income: Its Measurement, Determination and Relation to Public Policy*. New York: Holt, Rinehart and Winston, Inc., 1963.

Survey of Current Business. (For current national income and product data. Latest revisions are discussed in the August 1965 issue.)

United Nations, *A System of National Accounts and Supporting Tables*. New York: Department of Economic and Social Affairs, 1964.

Economic Analysis

*Ackley, Gardner, *Macroeconomic Theory*. New York: Macmillan, 1960.

*Allen, R. G. D., *Macro Economic Theory*. London: St. Martin's.

*Bailey, Martin J., *National Income and the Price Level*. New York: McGraw-Hill, 1962.

*Chandler, Lester V., *The Economics of Money and Banking*, 4th ed. New York: Harper & Row, 1964.

*Dernburg, Thomas F. and Duncan M. McDougall, *Macroeconomics: The Measurement, Analysis and Control of Aggregate Economic Activity*, 3d ed. New York: McGraw-Hill, 1968.

Domar, Evsey. "Capital Expansion, Rate of Growth, and Employment," *Econometrica*, vol. 14 (1946) p. 137–147.

Friedman, Milton and Anna J. Schwartz, *A Monetary History of the United States, 1867–1960*. New York: National Bureau of Economic Research, Inc., 1963.

Friedman, Milton, ed., *Studies in the Quantity Theory of Money*. Chicago: University of Chicago Press, 1956.

Gurley, John G. and Edward S. Shaw, *Money in a Theory of Finance*. Washington, D.C.: Brookings, 1960.
Harrod, Roy F., "An Essay in Dynamic Theory," *Economic Journal*, vol. 49 (1939) pp. 14–33.
Hendershott, Patric H., *The Neutralized Money Stock*. Homewood, Ill.: Irwin, 1968.
Horwich, George, *Money, Capital and Prices*. Homewood, Ill.: Irwin, 1964.
*McKenna, Joseph P. *Aggregate Economic Analysis*, rev. ed. New York: Holt, Rinehart and Winston, Inc., 1965.
*Moore, Basil J., *An Introduction to the Theory of Finance*. New York: Free Press, 1968.
Patinkin, Don, *Money, Interest, and Prices*, 2d ed. New York: Harper & Row, 1965.
*Peterson, Wallace C., *Income, Employment, and Economic Growth*, rev. ed. New York: Norton, 1962.
*Pesek, Boris P. and Thomas R. Saving, *Money, Wealth, and Economic Theory*. New York: Macmillan, 1967.
Samuelson, Paul A., "The Simple Mathematics of Income Determination" in *Income, Employment, and Public Policy: Essays in Honor of Alvin H. Hansen*. New York: Norton, 1948.
Tobin, James, *National Economic Policy*. New Haven, Conn.: Yale University Press, 1966.

Finite Mathematics

There are several excellent introductions to matrix theory. For purposes of this text, however, the simpler discussions in textbooks of finite mathematics are adequate. Readers are referred to:

*Kattsoff, L. O. and A. J. Simone, *Finite Mathematics with Applications in the Social and Management Sciences*. New York: McGraw-Hill, 1965.
*Kemeny, John, J. L. Snell, and G. L. Thompson, *Introduction to Finite Mathematics*, 2d ed. Englewood Cliffs, N.J.: Prentice-Hall, 1966.

INDEX